A Faith
You Can
Live With

The **Come & See Series** from Sheed & Ward is modeled on Jesus' compassionate question: "What do you seek?" and his profound invitation to "Come and see" the world through the eyes of faith (John 1:38–39). The series offers spiritual seekers lively, thought-provoking, and accessible books that explore topics of faith and the Catholic Christian tradition. Each book in the series is written by trustworthy guides who are the very best teachers, theologians, and scholars.

Series Editors: James Martin, S.J.
Jeremy Langford

A Faith
You Can
Live With

**Understanding
the Basics**

John O'Donnell, S.J.

SHEED & WARD
Franklin, Wisconsin

As an apostolate of the Priests of the Sacred Heart, a Catholic religious order, the mission of Sheed & Ward is to publish books of contemporary impact and enduring merit in Catholic Christian thought and action. The books published, however, reflect the opinions of their authors and are not meant to represent the official position of the Priests of the Sacred Heart.

1999

Sheed & Ward
7373 South Lovers Lane Road
Franklin, Wisconsin 53132
1-800-Booklog (1-800-266-5564)

Printed in the United States of America

Cover and interior design: Biner Design and GrafixStudio, Inc.

Cover art: "Green Place in the City" by Ansgar Holmberg, CSJ, St. Paul, Minnesota

Scripture quotations are from the Revised Standard Version of the Bible, copyright 1946, 1952, and 1971 by the Division of Christian Education of the National Council of the Churches of Christ in the USA. Used by permission. All rights reserved.

Excerpts from the English translation of the *Catechism of the Catholic Church* for use in the United States of America Copyright © 1994, United States Catholic Conference, Inc.—*Liberia Editrice Vaticana*. Used with permission.

Library of Congress Cataloging-in-Publication Data
O'Donnell, John J. (John Joseph), 1944-
    A faith you can live with: understanding the basics / by John O'Donnell.
        p. cm. – (Come & see)
      ISBN 1-58051-065-5 (alk. paper)
      1.   Catholic Church – Doctrines. I. Title. II. Series.
    BX1751.2 .0295   1999
    248.4'82 – dc21   99-16885
                                                                    CIP

1 2 3 4 5 / 02 01 00 99

Contents

For Tom and Ray

Preface

I have written this book for college-educated men and women who have no formal training in theology. Over many years of offering retreats for and teaching adult education programs to lay Catholics, I have been bombarded by important questions concerning the faith. These questions frequently have included inquiries as to what could be read as follow-up material for deepening the faith. I have often found myself at a loss to suggest good reading. Most of what I am familiar with from theology is too technical for a lay audience.

In writing this book, then, I have tried to steer a middle course between two different approaches. The first approach was to write a strictly theological text, using the technical language of theology and offering appropriate scholarly footnotes. The second approach was to present something like a catechism. The recently published *Catechism of the Catholic Church* offers a comprehensive approach to the Catholic faith—everything one could possibly want to know about Catholicism is included—but it lacks a synthetic vision. My study offers a synthesis that I hope will help interested readers gain access to the Catholic tradition. I do not pretend that the reader will find an answer to every question, but I do hope that my study will offer a solid foundation to what Christian faith is all about.

Although I have been studying theology in a formal way for over twenty-five years, I did not want my study to be a technical one. I have written this book from the heart, working from my own insights and prayer over the years, with roughly nothing in front of me but the Bible. If my approach has anything special to commend it, it may be that it tries to offer a spiritual vision of the faith. I have tried to treat every aspect of the faith from a spiritual angle, asking how the issue in question can guide a Christian to lead a "life in the Spirit." I have tried to write in a way that will inspire men and women today to believe.

The first part of this study is concerned with the doctrines of faith as they are found in the Apostles' Creed, the primary declaration of what Catholics believe. I also include a section on the sacraments, since these form an important part of Catholic life. The rest of the book is concerned with aspects of the faith that are more ordered to prayer, worship, and Christian life. Contemporary Jesuit historian John O'Malley has taught me the danger of over-intellectualizing the faith. The meaning of faith is not found just in what Christians believe but in how they pray and live. The devotional life of Christians is an important clue to the meaning of faith. O'Malley calls this "Christianitas," which refers to not only the doctrines of faith but also the lived practice of faith in all its richness. A large part of this study is devoted to Christianitas.

I have often thought of this study as "the Word of Life," which comes from the first letter of John 1:1. The expression appeals to me because it is Christ-centered and puts the accent on life. Christian faith is meant to give us life. We believe because we are convinced that faith gives meaning and vivacity to our lives.

This book is offered as a type of primer of Christian faith. Throughout Christian history teachers of the faith have offered works of catechesis, or instruction. One thinks, for example, of Hippolytus (c. 170–236) and his *Apostolic Tradition,* in which he passes on the church's early liturgical texts; and of the catechetical instructions of noted Church Father Cyril of Jerusalem (c. 315–386). Especially at the time of the Reformation, the sixteenth-century upheaval that divided the Western Christian Church into Catholic and Protestant, teachers of the faith wrote so-called "Primers of Faith." Because the Reformation was a time of division, the different confessions sought to draw the lines of belief. These primers were written primarily for children but, in fact, often served adults as well, especially catechists, those responsible for teaching the Christian faith. Our age, fortunately, is more ecumenical and hence more irenic; in other words, the churches are seeking ways to heal their divisions. Still, there is a great ignorance and indeed confusion about the faith. It is my sincere hope that this primer will help those individuals who are searching for faith or want to know their faith better. As has been true through the millennia, the Holy Spirit continues to mission us to preach the good news of Christ, who remains the Word of Life for the future as well as the past.

The Apostles' Creed

I believe in God the Father almighty,
*   creator of heaven and earth.*
And in Jesus Christ, his only son, our Lord.
*   He was conceived by the Holy Spirit, born of the*
*   Virgin Mary,*
*   suffered under Pontius Pilate, was crucified, died, and*
*   was buried.*
*   He descended into hell*
*   and on the third day he rose again from the dead.*
*   He ascended into heaven and is seated at the right hand*
*   of the Father.*
*   He will come again to judge the living and the dead.*

I believe in the Holy Spirit,
    the holy catholic Church,
    the communion of saints,
    the forgiveness of sins,
    the resurrection of the body and life everlasting.
Amen.

Christian faith is the surrender of the human person to God in Christ. But Christian faith is not only a human act; faith also has content based on what God has done for human beings in Christ and in his Spirit. Articles of faith express the content of the Christian faith. One beautiful summary of the articles of faith is the Apostles' Creed.

Although legend suggests that the Apostles' Creed derives from the apostles themselves, historical scholarship has shown that this is not the case. The earliest existent text of the Creed dates to the eighth century, and references to it go back to the fourth century. As early as the fifth century, the Apostles' Creed formed part of the baptismal initiation and was used in the instruction of people who were becoming Christians.

The Creed itself has a *trinitarian* structure; it reflects a faith in the Trinity—God the Father, God the Son, and God the Holy Spirit. The first article refers to God the Father and creator. The second article refers to Christ's life, death, and resurrection. The third article deals with the Holy Spirit and the presence of the Spirit in the church. The Creed concludes with Christian hope in the resurrection and life everlasting.

The Apostles' Creed is beautiful for its succinct biblical language. The Apostles' Creed differs in this respect from other creeds, such as the Nicene Creed which dates to the fourth century and expands the events of salvation history with theological language and philosophical expressions. The Apostles' Creed is used in this book because of its simplicity. In brief formulas, it contains the heart of Christian faith. We will comment on each article of the Creed, interpreting the text line by line.

I believe in God
the Father almighty

The Apostles' Creed begins with a personal confession of faith—faith being an act that involves our whole being. According to noted German Protestant theologian Paul Tillich (1886–1965), faith is the centered act of the personality. In other words, we cannot commit ourselves by half-measures in the act of faith. In faith, we make a total surrender to God.

The word *surrender* here is key. Faith is not primarily an intellectual act; it is not the simple acceptance of a set of doctrines. Rather, faith involves a personal commitment. It is an act of trust in which we hand over our lives to God. That is why faith is radically simple. Although the church over the centuries has explicated the Christian faith in ever-greater detail, God always remains the heart of faith. The articles of the Creed merely help us understand more fully the God to whom we surrender. Theologians may spill a lot of ink trying to understand the faith and show its reasonability but, in the end, we always come back to our simple surrender to God.

In the Catholic tradition, faith has always been acknowledged as a gift. Human intelligence can show that faith is reasonable, and history can offer solid grounds for believing in God's revelation in Israel and in Jesus. But faith can never be coerced. Men and women do not stand before the faith of the church as mere neutral observers. Rather, they come with their most burning desires, their human hungers, and their questions of meaning. In biblical language, they are searching for eternal life. It is God's grace that allows men and women to assent to faith—and it is only God who brings them to believe and to surrender their lives. As Jesus said, "No one can come to me unless the Father who sent me draw him" (John 6:44).

In this first affirmation of the Creed we dare to use the word *God*. God is one of the most mysterious words in human language, a word often overloaded with connotations that can actually impede belief. So difficult has the word *God* become in modern culture that the great Jewish theologian Martin Buber (1878–1965), noted for his work on the prophets, suggested that we ban it from our human vocabulary altogether. But this approach will not work. The word *God* is too much a part of human culture. Rather, we must ask what the word *God* means.

Karl Rahner (1904–1984), the Jesuit theologian who helped prepare the Second Vatican Council (1962–1965), offered an excellent suggestion when he referred to God as "holy Mystery"—not mystery in the sense of something enigmatic or puzzling, however, for God is full of intelligibility. Rather, God is so infinitely luminous that we can never fully grasp him. God is per force the elusive presence. God is not an object in our world. If he were an object, then God would not be God; rather, God would be something finite. If God is Mystery, however, we can never fully grasp or master him; God always remains, in some sense, beyond us. Should this fact overwhelm us or make us angry? No. God's mysterious Being means that we can only approach God through the exercise of our human freedom. Rahner has observed that we cannot control God; we cannot put God in our pockets, so to speak; we cannot master the infinite God. But another way is open to us—to freely entrust our lives, in love, to a loving God. The greatest act of freedom possible to us as human beings is a loving response to God. The way to God is not through mastery but through the freedom of surrender.

Rahner also says that philosophy leads us to a distant God. We may know that there is an Absolute or Cause of the universe, but this knowledge is not salvific. In other words, knowing this is not, in and of itself, saving or redeeming. What we desperately want to know is whether this God is interested in us, whether this God wishes to enter into relationship with us.

Here is where faith comes into play. The God of the Bible is a God of relationship, a God who chooses to draw near to us. The biblical word for this is *covenant*. God chooses a people, Israel, to be special, and the covenant that God begins with Israel comes to its fulfillment when God sends the Son to be the new and eternal covenant. Thus in the Old Testament we read the moving words, "I will put my spirit within you, and cause you to walk in my statutes and be careful to observe my ordinances. You shall dwell in the land which I gave to your fathers and you shall be my people and I will be your God" (Ezekiel 36: 27–28). And in the New Testament, John begins his Gospel with the prologue that culminates with these words: "[T]he Word became flesh and dwelt amongst us, full of grace and truth, and we have seen his glory, glory as of the only Son from the Father" (1:14). Notice, as we so often do in the Gospels, that these words are a profound echo of the Old Testament. The glory of God is the manifestation of God's divinity. When God makes himself known in history, what appears is God's radiance and splendor. For John there is no greater revelation of the divine beauty than in the Incarnation of the Son. Although God's glory is manifested in the theophany—an appearance or manifestation of God—on Mount Sinai in the Old Testament, and the prophets are often given intimations of the divine glory, Jesus is the theophany of God's majesty *par excellence.*

John goes on to use two important words to describe Jesus; Jesus is the manifestation of the divine *grace* and the divine *truth.* The Greek word for grace, *charis,* reflects back on the Old Testament words for the divine mercy. *Mercy* is one of the key words used to describe the God of the covenant. God makes a covenant with Israel for no other motive than love: "It was not because you were more in number than any other people that the Lord set his love upon you and chose you, for you were the fewest of all peoples; but it is because the Lord loves you" (Deuteronomy 7:7–8).

The Hebrew language actually has a number of words to express the divine mercy. One word is *rahamin,* which derives from the word that means "womb." A mother always has compassion for the child of her womb. So, too, God's love for Israel—God's people, God's offspring—is a compassionate love. A famous passage in Isaiah suggests this: "Can a woman forget her sucking child, that she should have no compassion on the son of her womb? Even these may forget yet I will not forget you" (49:15).

Another key word for mercy is the Hebrew word *hesed.* Pope John Paul II's letter titled *Rich in Mercy* has a footnote on the word *hesed,* explaining that it implies an inner bond between two parties. In the patriarchal culture of the East, for example, a man shows hesed when he chooses a girl as his bride. It is a free choice on his part but, by choosing her, he binds himself interiorly. Such is God's relationship with Israel; God is truly committed to the covenant relationship.

Thus it is obvious that the divine mercy and the divine fidelity go together. God remains faithful in mercy and in so doing is faithful to himself. A constant refrain of the Psalms in the Old Testament is praise of God's fidelity: "For his great love is without end" (Psalm 136). Admittedly, the people of Israel pressed God's faithful love to the limit in times of great infidelity and, occasionally, came close to believing that God would abandon them. But God remained faithful—the ultimate sign of this fidelity being Jesus Christ. As we saw above, John speaks of Jesus as "full of truth." Truth is that which can be relied upon, that which will last, hold up, give support. It is God who is our ultimate support. We build our lives on God's fidelity. Again, this is beautifully expressed in a brief passage in 2 Timothy: "If we have died with him, we shall also live with him; if we endure, we shall also reign with him; if we deny him, he will also deny us; if we are faithless, he remains faithful—for he cannot deny himself" (2:11–13).

Let us now turn our attention briefly to the final word in our opening confession of faith: *Father*. Hebrew faith went to great lengths to avoid attributing biological traits to God. The Canaanite religion, with which Israel came into contact, was a goddess religion, and fertility was a key feature of the pagan gods. Israelite monotheism, of course, firmly rejected this notion. Hence, the Hebrews were reluctant to speak of God as "father" or "mother."

Thus God is not generally prayed to as "father" in the Old Testament. Yet, there are a few moving references to the divine fatherhood. For the most part, these are found in the prophets and were developed around the time of the Exile (587 B.C.), when Jerusalem and its Tmeple were destroyed and the Hebrews were forced to flee to Babylonia. Precisely at this time, when Israelite faith was profoundly tested, the prophets appealed to the tender image of God as father. We find a moving example in Hosea: "When Israel was a child I loved him, and out of Egypt I called my son. . . . Yet it was I who taught Ephraim to walk, I took them up in my arms; but they did not know that I healed them. I led them with cords of compassion, with the bands of love, and I became to them as one who eases the yoke on their jaws, and I bent down to them and fed them" (11:1–4).

In the New Testament, however, God as father has a high profile. One of the most striking novelties in the ministry of Jesus, in fact, is his unique way of praying; the word *Father* is constantly on his lips. The New Testament gives three examples of the word *Abba,* the Aramaic word for "father" that conveys intimacy and trust (see Mark 14:36, Romans 8:15, and Galatians 4:6). The explicit use of this Aramaic word in the New Testament—Aramaic being the language Jesus himself used—suggests that we are in touch with a solid fact of Jesus' life: He prayed to his God as *Abba.* He had a relationship with God of great intimacy and trust, and he invites us, his disciples, into that same type of relationship. It is noteworthy that one place where Jesus refers to God as Father is in the garden of Gethsemane just before his arrest. Jesus thus perseveres in loving trust in God even in the moment of extreme trial—when he is not spared suffering and God seems totally absent. We are invited to do the same.

Calling upon God as Father is therefore a way of expressing our trust as we surrender our lives to God. By calling God Father and by praying to God as Father, for example in the Lord's Prayer, we are expressing our discipleship and appropriating in our lives Jesus' relationship to God. Paul sums this up beautifully in Galatians when he says, "God has poured the Spirit of his Son into our hearts, crying Abba! Father!" (4:6)

In speaking of God as Father we do not mean, of course, that God is literally father. God does not have gender as we do. Rather "Father" is a metaphor for expressing God's tenderness, desire, and providential care for us.

Today, in light of feminism, the Fatherhood of God has become problematic. The symbol of fatherhood for many women causes pain, especially for women who have been victims of abuse. Although I do not believe that we can abandon this image of God since it is so tightly linked to Jesus, his mission, and his way of praying, I do agree that we have to remember how Jesus broke with many patriarchal traditions and customs. He was especially close to women, and women felt uniquely comfortable and safe in his presence. When we pray "Our Father," we affirm Jesus' attitude toward God and make it our own. Such prayer, however, does not deny the gentle mother image of God. Moreover, Jesus' attitude requires that we respect and affirm the gifts of women.

We must remember, too, that the Bible contains many images for God. In addition to king, shepherd, and spouse, for example, there are some beautiful feminine images as well. We have already seen an example of motherhood in the Old Testament (see Isaiah 49:15). There is also the whole Old Testament tradition of Wisdom, the divine Sophia, portrayed as a woman who takes to the streets in search of her children (see Proverbs 1:20). Then there are moving New Testament images, such as the woman resolutely looking everywhere for her lost coin (see Luke 14:8–10). A biblical approach to God, therefore, leaves room for us to see God not only as our father but also as our mother, a God who gives us life and a God who is full of tenderness and compassion.

...creator of heaven and earth

The central tenet of Israel's belief lies in her conviction of divine election. God chose Israel to be a special people, a people of destiny. No words are more important in the Old Testament than these of the prophet Ezekiel: "You will be my people and I will be your God" (36:28). In the Book of Deuteronomy, Israel—the tiniest of peoples, with no particular claim to merit or importance—meditates upon the gratuity of God's choice. It is only because of God's inscrutable love that she becomes the people of election.

The central event in the story of Israel's relationship with God is the Exodus—the deliverance of Israel from slavery in Egypt. God chose Moses to lead his people out of slavery into the promised land. When God calls Moses to this special mission, he reveals his name as *Yahweh,* a complicated Hebrew word that is often translated "I am who am." The mysterious character of the word points to God's mysterious Being. Some scholars think that the sense of the word might be "I will make happen what happens."

It seems clear that at the time of the Exodus, the Jewish people were not monotheists in the strictest sense; they had their powerful God, Yahweh, just as other tribes or nations had their gods. Eventually, however, Israel came to see that Yahweh was so powerful that no other god existed besides him. It was especially under the influence of the prophets that Israel came to a strict monotheism.

I mention this history because it helps us understand the development of faith in God the creator. The more Israel reflects on her experience of God, the clearer it becomes that God is not just the God of Israel but is, in fact, the only God there is. This God is the Lord of the cosmos, the sovereign God of everything. In short, God is the creator, the Lord of heaven and earth.

Philip Rosato, a brother Jesuit who is a theologian, has suggested that every article of faith has four dimensions: each article of faith *refers to reality*; each touches the believer's *personal existence*; each has *social* (communal) *consequences*; and each contains a dimension of *human hope*.

Turning to the first point we ask, "What does faith in God the creator tell us about *reality*? What does it tell us about the world we live in?" Believing in God as the creator is believing that everything is in God's hands; every creature in the world comes from God. There is absolutely nothing that can in any way compete with God.

This immediately leads us to the second dimension of every article of faith: the *personal experience* or meaning. Here we ask what significance "belief in God the creator" has for our lives. What difference does it make to our everyday lives to believe in a creator God? The answer is that we can totally trust in God because we know we are in God's hands.

Fundamentally, we face an alternative between two choices in our human lives: We can try to make ourselves God, believing that we can control reality and manipulate it for our own purposes—*or* we can surrender to God in loving trust. The first is pride; the second is humility. Humility does not mean a groveling attitude of abasement. Humility comes from the Latin word *humus*, which means "ground." We humans are of the earth. As the psalmist says, we are made of dust (see Psalm 103:14). This could cause a deflating attitude, of course, but it need not do so. Rather, this fact of "earthliness" can lead us to trust. We don't have to control everything; we can trust in God's care.

Our faith in Christ is intimately linked to our faith in the creator. In fact, in the New Testament, Christ is seen as the Word through whom God created. Moreover, since Christ has risen from the dead, we see him as victor over the powers of chaos and destruction. He has eternal life in himself. Nothingness has no hold on him. This is important on the personal level, for it means that Christ is omnipotent over anything that threatens to destroy us. Paul sums it up in a remarkable passage when he says in Romans that "Nothing can separate us from the love of God." He continues, " I am sure that neither death, nor life, nor angels, nor principalities, nor things present, nor things to come, nor powers, nor height, nor depth, nor anything else in all creation will be able to separate us from the love of God in Christ Jesus our Lord" (8:38–39).

A third dimension of the aspect of God the creator is the *social*, or communal, aspect. In the Book of Genesis, there are two accounts of creation (see Genesis 1:1–2:4b and 2:4b–3:24). The second relates the story of the creation of Adam and Eve. In the words of this creation account, God says, "It is not good that the man should be alone" (2:18). Hence, fellowship is an important part of being a creature, and the most sublime form of communion is that between man and woman.

Genesis 1:27 affirms that "God created man in his own image, in the image of God he created him; male and female he created them." Over the centuries theologians have debated just how this divine likeness is made manifest in the human person. Sometimes it was affirmed that the divine likeness is in human reason. But more profoundly, we could argue that our divine likeness consists in community. We have been made by God for love. When human beings live together in peace and harmony, they reflect the nature of God. Although the author of Genesis was not thinking explicitly about the Trinity, we know, through the revelation of Christ, that God is, in fact, a divine community where three equal and divine Persons love one another without reserve and share the divine life in common. The human family reflects this divine community and so is an image of the Trinity. In the divine Trinity the love of the Father and the Son overflows in an excess of love, bringing forth the Holy Spirit; love always contains a superabundant fruitfulness. In a similar way, the love of husband and wife overflows in the conception of the child. The child is not merely the child of the father or the child of the mother; rather, the child is their common offspring and the fruitfulness of their love. This fact also reflects the Trinity, where the Spirit is the Love of the Father and the Son. Saint Augustine of Hippo (354–430), bishop and one of the greatest thinkers and teachers of the

Western church, called the Spirit the bond of union between the Father and the Son.

Especially in the Old Testament, there are signs of a patriarchal worldview, where all rights reside in the man and the man has dominion over others, including women. But Genesis sees that man needs woman to be himself. Hence, in principle, the patriarchal point of view is overcome. We must read Genesis in light of the New Testament, which radicalizes the view of women by presenting them as equal to men and worthy of infinite dignity. As Paul says, "There is neither Jew nor Greek, there is neither slave nor free, there is neither male nor female; for you are all one in Christ Jesus" (Galatians 3:27).

Another possible danger of this patriarchal point of view can be found in God's command to the man to have dominion over the earth (see Genesis 1:28)—yet, God lets the man name the animals (see Genesis 2:20). Scripture scholars see in this gesture an invitation by God to share in the work of creation. Today, biblical scholars emphasize that to see humanity as being charged by God with the total domination of the world is a false reading of the Bible. Rather, human beings are called to stewardship. The cosmos is given to humankind for its cultivation, not its exploitation. We are stewards rather than rulers of the earth.

Finally, we come to the hope dimension of the doctrine of creation. Our belief in the creator God is linked to not only the world's beginnings but also to the fulfillment of God's plan. This aspect of faith reminds us that all our Christian beliefs are related to our final human hopes. Thus it is important to remember that creation concerns not only the beginning but also the end.

We have already indicated that God created in and through Christ. This fact reminds us that the future of creation is nothing less than the restoration of all things in Christ. The end will be more than the beginning, for in the end we shall be fully incorporated into Christ's Sonship and will share with him in the glory of the Father.

The New Testament has many beautiful images for this. In the Book of Revelation, for example, we read: "I saw a new heaven and a new earth; for the first heaven and the first earth had passed away" (21:1). The author then proceeds to describe the heavenly Jerusalem: "The dwelling of God is with men. He shall dwell with them, and they shall be his people . . . God will wipe away every tear from their eyes, and death shall be no more, neither shall there be mourning, nor crying, nor pain any more, for the former things have passed away" (21:3–4).

This, then, is the fulfillment of Christ's mission. The new creation, begun with his resurrection, is brought to completion. Sickness, suffering, mourning, and death are definitively overcome. We will be with Christ in the kingdom of his

Father. The work begun in the creation will be complete. Paul, speaking in the same vein and writing in the context of Christ's surpassing victory, sees the end in these terms: "God will be everything to everyone" (1 Corinthians 15:28).

The Book of Genesis says that on the seventh day God rested from creating. In imitation of this rest, the Jewish people were commanded by God to celebrate the weekly Sabbath. The Sabbath was of critical importance to remind human beings that work is not the goal of human life; rather, the goal is rest with God. Work must ultimately give way to play, the purposeless activity of lovers who enjoy being in each other's presence. This message is more urgent today than ever before, especially in a culture that measures everything by efficiency and marketability. We are losing the values of play, friendship, and rest for their own sakes. The Christian Sabbath can help us revive these values.

The resurrection is the beginning of the eternal Sabbath. The Church Fathers, the great theologians of the early centuries of the church, often called the day of the resurrection "the eighth day of creation." The first Sabbath was a prelude to the second, to the feast of Easter. Each Sunday is a little Easter, a reminder that we are created for life and that one day we shall enjoy life to the full, life without end, in the presence of Christ and his Father.

And in Jesus Christ, his only Son, our Lord

This is considered the second article of the Creed. In the famous opening verse of the letter to the Hebrews, the author confesses, "In many and various ways God spoke of old to our fathers by the prophets; but in these last days he has spoken to us by a Son." The Mystery of God has been revealed to us and has drawn close to us in the history of Israel, but God's revelation reaches its unsurpassable climax in the coming of his Son Jesus. It is not that God does not wish to say anything further to us. Rather, God has expressed his very Being in complete fullness in Jesus Christ. God is given to us in Jesus with the unreservedness of prodigal love.

The source and goal of our human pilgrimage of faith is the Father—but the way to the Father is his Son. In those unforgettable and audacious words, Jesus declared himself to be "the Way, the Truth and the Life" (John 14:6). Has any person ever spoken in this way or made such claims for himself or herself? If the Old Testament in the Law offered human beings a path to God and a way of life, the New Testament offers a path that is a person—none other than the beloved Son of God.

The three central words of our confession of faith—Christ, Son, and Lord—are echoed in the Gospel of Luke in the angelic proclamation to the shepherds at the birth of Jesus: "For to you is born this day in the city of David a Savior who is Christ the Lord" (2:11). This brief verse contains in nucleus our entire faith in Jesus as revelation of the Father.

It is common for Christians to say that they believe in "Jesus Christ." In this declaration, however, the two words, *Jesus* and *Christ*, have been so linked together in Christian tradition and prayer that they appear to represent one name. The word *Christ*, however, is a title given to Jesus. It is one of the earliest confessions about Jesus, one that grew up in the soil of Judaism. Our English word *Christ* derives from the Greek word *Christos*, which means "anointed one." In Judaism both the king and the high priest were anointed. Christians came to see Christ as both the King of Israel and the eternal High Priest.

The traditions around the Jewish king or messiah are complex. For example, although there was an anointed king on the throne for much of Jewish history—men such as David and Solomon—most of these kings were condemned by the prophets for their scurrilous personal lives and general unfaithfulness to the Law. Still, the figure of the ideal king was always important to Jewish belief. In hard times, especially during and after the Exile, for example, the hope of a new ideal king was strong. Later, at the time of the birth of Jesus, Israel was living under the yoke of Roman oppression and messianic hopes were stirred. This fact inspired the zealot movement that sought to overcome Roman occupation by force. According to the Gospels, some of Jesus' disciples were zealots.

Many Jewish contemporaries looked for the coming of the Messiah, one who was understood to be a human figure but of noble and idealized features. As suggested above, the Messiah was often thought to be a military figure. Jesus' conception was totally different, of course, so he was seen as a contradiction. That Jesus was understood to be the Messiah, however, is confirmed by the title over his cross—"The King of the Jews"—and with time this title gained a new spiritual meaning. Other titles, such as "Lord," actually became much more important to the faith as the gospel spread into the Greek world.

For our own faith, we might gain a better understanding of the kingship of Jesus by looking at the question of suffering and oppression. The disciples of John the Baptist went to Jesus with the question, "Are you he who is to come or shall we look for another?" (Luke 7:19) Like these disciples, men and women have always looked for the one who would come, the one who would free them from suffering, death, oppression, and injustice. Christian faith sees that person in Jesus.

It is clear from all the gospel accounts that Jesus heals people—from physical infirmities as well as from spiritual illness. Mark, for example, portrays Jesus as one who has the power to overcome even the forces of Satan. We see this in chapter five, where Jesus frees a man possessed of many demons. The man is so possessed that he goes about looking wild, runs naked, and breaks the chains of those who seek to hold him in check. Yet, when Jesus exorcizes him, the man appears calm, serene, fully clothed, a model of a man fully at peace with himself and God (see 1–20). Surely Mark wishes to say that Jesus offers each of us, his disciples, that same possibility.

Christian hymns speak of Jesus as "King of love on Calvary," manifesting his power in the powerlessness of love. He is victorious over evil on the cross; death does not defeat him. But when Jesus is raised from the dead, he bears the marks of his crucifixion in his body. Hence, the kingship of Jesus is intrinsically linked to his cross. We are promised victory with Christ but only if we pass through his death to resurrection with him. Christian victory over suffering and death can only take place through the cross. This truth, too, is at the heart of Mark's Gospel. There we see Peter as the first to recognize Jesus as the Messiah and, from the moment of Peter's confession of faith, Jesus' entire energy goes into explaining the meaning of his messianic identity. The confession that

Jesus is Messiah is immediately followed by the prediction of his suffering and death.

We now consider the word Son in this confession of faith. Here, too, we confront a rich heritage from the Old Testament. The Psalms, for example, speak of the king as "God's son," suggesting clearly that the phrase *Son of God* in the Bible has more than one meaning.

For our purposes, we focus on the personal relationship between Jesus and his Father. We already reflected on this when speaking of Jesus' way of praying to God as *Abba*. Another dimension of Jesus' Sonship is the intimate knowledge that Jesus has of God and of God's plan of salvation. A well-known saying in Matthew's Gospel brings home this point: "All things have been delivered to me by my Father; and no one knows the Son except the Father, and no one knows the Father except the Son and anyone to whom the Son chooses to reveal him" (11:27). Jesus lives in extraordinary intimacy with the Father. He knows the Father's plan of salvation, reveals this to us, and invites us to enter into his relationship as Son.

In the Fourth Gospel, John uses the notion of Jesus' Sonship as a recurring theme. He sums up the whole gospel message when he affirms: "God so loved the world that he gave his only begotten Son, that whoever believes in him should not perish but have eternal life" (3:16).

What most impresses me when I think of this image of Jesus as beloved Son is the personal bond of intimate love that Jesus has with God. In that image, I hear Jesus inviting me into this intimacy. John's Gospel seeks ever-new ways to help us understand this truth. In the tenth chapter, for example, John speaks of Jesus as shepherd; the shepherd pastures the sheep and even lays down his life for the flock. But perhaps most important for John is the fact that the sheep know the shepherd and recognize his voice. The great promise of Jesus is: "I know my own and my own know me" (10:14). In knowing Jesus we are bonded not only with him but also with his Father.

Toward the end of his Gospel, in the Last Supper discourse, John goes to even greater lengths to unpack for us the meaning of this intimacy. The knowledge between Jesus and the disciple is not merely an external one. Rather, Jesus and the Father come to dwell within the believer. The ultimate bonds of union between God and Jesus go deeper than any human analogy can suggest, even the sexual one. The Father is in Jesus and Jesus is in us by the gift of the Holy Spirit. Hence, the mystery of Jesus' Sonship is, in the final analysis, the mystery of the divine indwelling: "I in them and thou in me" (John 17:23).

We also confess Jesus to be Lord, which is an extraordinary affirmation of faith, for it is equivalent to calling Jesus

"God." Indeed, in the Fourth Gospel, that is exactly Thomas's confession of faith before the risen Jesus: "My Lord and my God" (20:28).

It was a bold adventure when the early Christian communities began to apply the divine word *Kyrios* (Lord) to Jesus. It is certainly remarkable when we reflect on how rigorous the Jewish faith was in preserving monotheism and excluding anything that would seem to compromise the one God of Israel. Scholars think that the path to this confession of faith may lie in Psalm 110:1: "The Lord said to my Lord, Sit at my right hand, until I place my enemies under your feet." The early church applied this psalm to the risen Christ, where God the Father says these words to his Son. In any case, the first Christian communities gradually began to see that Jesus is Lord and on the same level as the God of the Old Testament. This faith is reflected in various speeches in the Acts of the Apostles—for example, in Peter's words, "God has made him both Lord and Christ, this Jesus whom you crucified" (2:36).

As all confessions of faith, our calling Jesus *Lord* is no mere theoretical truth. Rather, this confession of faith is a summons to let Jesus be the Lord of our lives. Once again Paul can be our guide: "If you confess with your lips that Jesus is Lord and believe in your heart that God raised him from the dead, you will be saved" (Romans 10:9).

Believing that Jesus is Lord means surrendering our lives to him. He has conquered sin and death; he is risen; and he is with us each day. He accompanies us, holds us in his hands, and has sovereignty over our lives. And so the Lord Jesus asks us to surrender to him, to believe in him, to hand our lives over to him in trust. Faith in the Lord Jesus is this daily surrender of our lives not just in prayer but in the concrete circumstances of everyday life: in business and work, in family and friendship, in politics and statecraft. The challenge of faith is to confess the lordship of Jesus from day to day as we live in the world. This can be as ordinary as raising a family or as heroic as giving one's life, as did twentieth-century martyrs Dietrich Bonhoeffer (Protestant theologian martyred by the Nazis in 1945) and Oscar Romero (archbishop of San Salvador and defender of the rights of the poor; murdered by the military in El Salvador in 1980).

He was conceived by the Holy Spirit, born of the Virgin Mary

This article of the Creed deals with the birth of Jesus. As we shall note in the section on the resurrection, the earliest proclamation of the church had to do with Christ's being raised from the dead. It was only later that the community seemed to take a great interest in Jesus' birth.

We have significant material about the infancy of Jesus in the Gospels, particularly in the first two chapters of Matthew and Luke. Scripture scholars tell us that the Gospels were written in the 80s, some fifty years after the death of Jesus. Thus, although these stories in the Gospels contain some biographical information, such as the birth of Jesus in Bethlehem, the authors are not primarily interested in writing biography. Rather, they are proclaiming who Jesus is. The stories of the birth of Jesus are "gospel," in that they proclaim the good news, namely the birth of the Messiah of Israel. Thus as we look at this article of the Creed, we should be asking: What is this article trying to tell us about our faith? What aspect of Jesus is it proclaiming to us as being of great importance for our salvation?

We start with noting that in this article of the Creed, the church proclaims something about Jesus' conception. It says two things: Jesus had no human father, and the conception took place in the power of the Holy Spirit.

Jesus had no human father. This fact is proclaimed in both the Gospel of Luke and the Gospel of Matthew. Mary asks the angel in Luke's Gospel, "How shall this be since I have no husband?" (1:34) In Matthew's Gospel the Evangelist sees in the virginal conception of Jesus a fulfillment of the prophecy of Isaiah 7:14: "And a virgin shall conceive and bear a son, and his name shall be called Emmanuel" (1:23).

The Bible offers many stories of sterility. In the Old Testament, for example, we see Sarah, the mother of Isaac, and Hannah, the mother of Samuel. In the New Testament, there is Elizabeth, the mother of John the Baptist. All three women conceive in a normal way but they do so in old age. These biblical stories convey the power of God to effect salvation and redemption, even in what seems to be impossible situations.

This is all the more dramatically true in the case of the birth of Jesus. Mary is not old and barren; on the contrary, she is young and capable of childbearing. But she conceives, not through human intercourse, but through the power of the Holy Spirit. This Gospel proclamation says something about Mary but it is not primarily about Mary. It is a proclamation about God and what God can do.

Karl Barth (1886–1968), a great Protestant theologian of the twentieth century, once observed that two great signs of contradiction form bookends of a sort around the life of Jesus: the virginal conception and the empty tomb. Both represent the impossibility of human beings to save themselves. The human race, of its own, cannot produce a savior; neither can the dead raise themselves. But these two events point to the power of God: What is humanly impossible is possible by the omnipotent power of divine grace. As the angel says to Mary, "For with God nothing will be impossible" (Luke 1:37).

The Creed also says that Jesus was conceived by the power of the Holy Spirit, and in this, the Creed is pointing to two important truths. First, God is involved in the life of Jesus from the very beginning. The Gospels portray Jesus as the bearer of God's Spirit. But God's Spirit is with Jesus from the very beginning, not just at a later date, for example, at the moment of his baptism. No, Jesus is God's Son from the beginning. Jesus is led by God from the very first moment of his conception.

But there is also another truth that is alluded to here—the fact that Mary is overshadowed by the Spirit. Luke indicates this with the words of the angel Gabriel to Mary: "The Holy Spirit will come upon you, and the power of the Most High will overshadow you; therefore, the child to be born will be called holy, the Son of God" (1:35). These words echo the Old Testament, where God is present to Israel through the ark of the covenant. In Exodus we are told how a cloud covers the ark by day and a pillar of fire surrounds it by night (see chapter 14). The cloud and the fire indicate the presence of God. Since Mary is the new ark of the covenant, she, too, is overshadowed by the Holy Spirit because she bears the Son of God within her.

In the first chapter of Luke's Gospel we see the seeds of all future declarations of faith about Mary. The heart of the church's understanding of Mary is that she is virgin and mother. She conceives Jesus in her womb when she says "yes" to the divine plan, and her words echo through the ages: "Let it be done to me according to your word" (38). The Church Fathers taught that Mary conceived Christ in her heart by faith before she conceived him physically in her womb. Her virginal "yes" to God's plan produced an overwhelming fruitfulness in the divine maternity; she bore the Son of God.

The Gospel of John puts special emphasis on Mary's spiritual maternity. At the beginning of his Gospel, John narrates the story of the miracle of Cana. Mary commands the stewards to do what Jesus tells them. At her word, Jesus turns water into wine, a symbolic gesture that indicates the initiation of the wedding banquet of the messianic era. The wedding banquet begins at the invitation of Mary. Then on the cross, Jesus gives Mary, his mother, to the beloved disciple: "Behold your mother" (John 19:27). With these words John indicates that the Lord gives Mary to be the mother of all believers. The Second Vatican Council, the last great ecumenical council of church leaders, stressed the point that Mary is a symbol of the reality of the church. What she did by her "yes" we, too, must do by our "yes" to Christ in discipleship. And we, too, by the grace of baptism, participate in the motherhood of Mary. Christ is born in our hearts by the grace of eternal life. At the end of the council, Pope Paul VI (1897–1978), who completed the work of the Second Vatican Council and implemented its decrees, officially gave Mary the title "Mother of the Church."

The heart of the church's devotion to Mary lies in her virginity and motherhood. In 431, at the Council of Ephesus, the church formally declared Mary the Mother of God. She is the Mother of God because Jesus is the divine Son, indivisible in his being. In giving birth to Jesus, Mary gave birth to God-made-human.

In more recent times, the church made two more significant declarations about Mary. In 1854, Pope Pius IX (1792–1878), the pope who defended the church against increasing disbelief, declared that Mary was conceived immaculately (the Immaculate Conception) without original sin by a special grace of God. In 1950 Pope Pius XII (1876–1958), one of the most prominent of the twentieth-century popes, declared that Mary was assumed into heaven (the Assmption), both body and soul, and that her body did not undergo corruption.

These two dogmas are deeply rooted in the two biblical affirmations of Mary's virginity and divine motherhood. Mary was conceived immaculately to prepare her for her unique mission to be the Mother of God. God's providential grace was at work in her from the very first moment of her human existence, preparing her for that great moment when she would say "yes" to the divine plan for the salvation of all men and women. And just as grace is present in the beginning, so it is present at the end. Mary's death is not the death of sin, of separation from God. Rather, Mary, as the first of believers, is also the first to participate fully in the Lord's resurrection. Her yes of faith leads her to share in the Lord's glory.

In one sense, these are unique graces given to Mary for a unique vocation. But they are given to Mary so that all of us disciples can eventually be incorporated into them. Although we are not conceived immaculately, we are given eternal life in the font of baptism. And although we die and must wait the resurrection on the last day, we have the firm promise that we, too, like Mary, will rise one day in our bodies to share the risen life of Christ to the eternal praise of the Father. So the great graces we proclaim to be privileges of Mary are, at the same time, words of promise for all of us who, like Mary, believe in Christ.

...suffered under Pontius Pilate, was crucified, died, and was buried

It is interesting to note that the Creed jumps right from the birth of Jesus to his death, passing over his ministry. This is unfortunate since Jesus' ministry is motivated by his great sense of mission to preach the kingdom of God, to announce its imminent arrival, and to make it present in anticipatory fashion—through his healings, exorcisms, and dramatic gestures, such as eating with tax collectors and sinners and forgiving sins. In fact, the motive for Jesus' death lies in the provocative character of Jesus' claims about himself and in his prophetic gestures. For example, all the Gospels narrate the story of Jesus' cleansing of the Temple in Jerusalem. With this gesture, the community remembered a saying: "Destroy this temple and in three days I will build it up again" (John 2:19). John makes a link between this saying and Jesus' death. The Evangelist says that Jesus was talking about his body.

What seems clear, in any case, is that Jesus' ministry becomes a scandal to many people, especially the religious leaders. We must also remember that Israel lives under the domination of the occupying Roman power at that time; the country lives under Roman military rule and authority. Thus the prophetic nature of Jesus' ministry and the fact that he stirs the people no doubt arouses great fear in the religious leaders. Jesus can provoke a rebellion and, in this case, a terrible suppression could take place by the Romans. Such action would lead to vast bloodshed and to the end of the tenuous co-existence of Jews and Romans, whereby the Jews have a limited right to practice their religion. In fact, some forty years after the death of Jesus, such events do take place. The Romans destroy Herod's great Temple and the Jews are scattered in exile.

Our Creed says that Jesus suffers and is crucified under Pontius Pilate. These are true historical facts. The Jewish leaders hand Jesus over to the Roman authorities, who have the political power to execute a criminal. Pilate puts the title over the cross of Jesus: "The King of the Jews," so Jesus is executed as a political rebel. Because the Romans take him for one who wants to lead an armed insurrection, he is executed by a form of death that is both painfully excruciating and humiliating in its form; the naked body of the criminal is hoisted up for all to behold his shame. The Romans reserve this death for their most hated criminals.

From a Christian point of view, however, faith sees so much more in the death of Jesus than a political execution.

Faith sees a redemptive event. Especially important is that Jesus freely embraces his death, turning it into a self-offering for us.

The Gospels make it clear that Jesus sees his death approaching. He saw that prophets before him had been killed; he saw what happened to John the Baptist; he saw that the positive response to his message at the beginning of his ministry gradually diminished. The Gospels have as a constant theme the fact that the religious leaders sought to do away with Jesus. But in the face of this, as Luke tells us, Jesus decides to go to Jerusalem.

Just how Jesus comes to see interiorly the "necessity" of his death is a mystery. It seems clear, however, that he eventually sees that his death is part of God's plan. We see this in the prediction of his suffering and death. We see it also in the important saying of Jesus in Mark's Gospel: "The Son of Man came not to be served but to serve and give his life as a ransom for many" (10:45). We see it also in the institution of the Eucharist, where Jesus identifies the bread with his body that will be broken and given for many. We see it in the dramatic gesture of the foot-washing, when Jesus kneels before his disciples as their servant and washes their feet. But this gesture is only the prelude to the great gift on the next day at Calvary. John stresses the free character of the gift: "No one takes my life from me, but I lay it down of my own accord" (10:18).

Looking at Jesus' suffering and death, one might think that human characters such as Judas (see Luke 22), Caiphas (see Matthew 26), and Pilate (see Matthew 27) are the protagonists. Judas, for example, hands Jesus over in betrayal. But the Gospels make it clear that Jesus overturns the betrayal from within. Although he is betrayed from without, he makes the betrayal his own by handing himself over from within. All the Gospels reveal that in some sense Jesus is the protagonist of the suffering and death he endures—his gesture of forgiveness of the repentant thief in Luke (see 23:43), for example, and his dialogue with Pilate in John (see John 18). Jesus is the one who has true authority. In fact, all the symbolism around Jesus' suffering and death reveals that he is the true King.

Another important aspect of Jesus' death is the role of the Father. Naturally it would be wrong to see the Abba God of Jesus as directly willing the death of his Son. At the same time, the Father sends the Son into the world with a mission and the Father does not withdraw that mission even in the face of humankind's refusal of the Son. So we must come back in meditation to those important words of Paul in Romans 8:32: the Father "did not spare his own Son but gave him up for us all." And as we saw above, Jesus fully consents to this mission. Again Paul expresses it concisely when he writes, "He loved me and gave himself over for me" (Galatians 2:20).

The extent of this mutual "handing over" is seen in the abandonment of Christ on the cross. Both Mark and Matthew stress Jesus' dereliction on the cross. He dies with a loud cry and the words of Psalm 22 on his lips: "My God, my God, why hast thou forsaken me?" (1) Mark especially presents Jesus as the most abandoned of men, betrayed by Judas, abandoned by his disciples, and seemingly left in dereliction by the Father. Yet, the abandoned Jesus has always been a symbol of hope for the abandoned of the earth: for the slaves of human history, the victims of oppression and injustice, and contemporary abandoned ones such as those who suffer with AIDS. The risen Jesus, who still bears the marks of his death in his body, gives hope to all who feel abandoned.

On a theological level, we could say that Jesus on the cross tastes the full consequences of human sin, for what is sin but separation from self, others, and God? Of course, Jesus does not sin. He remains faithful. He lives to the end in fidelity to his being as Son. Luke expresses this in the words from the cross: "Into thy hands I commit my spirit" (23:46).

A number of contemporary theologians stress the trinitarian dimensions of the cross. All three Persons of the Trinity are involved in the cross event: the Father who hands over his Son, the Son who surrenders, and the Spirit who continues to unite the Father and the Son. The cross seems to be the moment of their greatest separation and yet, it is the moment of their greatest union, for it is an event of love—contrary to all appearances. A passage in the prophet Isaiah says that there was no beauty to behold in him (see Isaiah 53:2). But even the event of the cross can be said to be beautiful if we define beauty in terms of love.

Before we conclude this section of the Creed, we should note the final phrase: Jesus "was buried." Of course, this affirmation reflects the historical reality. The Gospels attest that Jesus is, in fact, buried. They even make reference to Joseph of Arimathea, who provides the tomb. But there is also a theological significance here. The burial points to the definitiveness of death; Jesus is sealed in the tomb—indicating death's finality—and history has never recorded anyone who has come back from the grave. From this perspective, the news of the resurrection takes on particular importance; what seems humanly impossible becomes a reality through the saving action of God—for the Father can raise him up.

He descended into hell

This declaration is almost entirely unintelligible to modern believers. It is inspired by a few enigmatic verses in the first letter of Peter, for example: "For Christ also died for sins once for all, the righteous for the unrighteous, that he might bring us to God, being put to death in the flesh but made alive in the spirit; in which he went and preached to the spirits in prison" (3:18–19) and "The gospel was preached even to the dead, that though judged in the flesh like men, they might live in the spirit like God" (4:6).

These verses convey the idea of a journey that Christ made to the underworld after his death. First, we should note that in no way does the author of 1 Peter intend to convey the idea of a descent of Christ to the hell of the damned. Rather, he is thinking in the categories of the Old Testament, that is, of the underworld that the Hebrews called Sheol.

The Jewish people did not have clear ideas about life after death. Only in the period immediately preceding the birth of Jesus did they begin to believe in the resurrection of the dead. Traditionally, they believed that the dead somehow survived death, but retained only a very shadowy existence in the underworld. The Psalms often speak of Sheol in various images, for example, as a land of silence, dust, and isolation, where the dead are not in solidarity with one another or with God. The predominant characteristic of Sheol is to be cut off from God, for God is the God of the living and not of the dead. In Psalm 6, we read, "In death there is no remembrance of thee, in Sheol who can give thee praise?" (5)

Christians presupposed these Jewish ideas of the underworld when they spoke of Christ's "descent." The problem was how to understand this descent in light of their belief in Christ's resurrection. The Christian tradition has thus interpreted "descended into hell" in two ways. Some theologians, extrapolating beyond what the Scripture says, have seen Christ's descent as a triumphal journey. Christ goes into the underworld to rescue the souls of the just, those who died before his birth and who hoped for a redeemer. If we think in this direction, we can correctly affirm that Christ's saving death is efficacious for all, even for the dead who lived before him. Christ's death reaches all. So the image of the decent of Christ among the dead would be a way of speaking of the salvation won for all by Christ's death.

But there is another line of thought, one that is perhaps more appropriate. Sheol, the underworld in the ancient way of thinking, represents the ultimate condition of human beings as sinners, human beings without Christ. Without the redeemer, we would be destined for death or a final separation from all that we hold dear—especially from God. Our final destiny would be ultimate aloneness. Our vocation to communion would be eternally frustrated.

Thus we can see Christ's death as an act of solidarity with sinners and with the human condition. The Gospels portray Jesus on the cross as abandoned. So one would see the descent into hell as a pictorial way of expressing Christ's solidarity with the ultimate depths to which human life is exposed. Christ descends into this fathomless abyss. His obedience to his mission and his desire to be in solidarity with us leads him even to this.

The descent into Sheol has to be linked, of course, to Jesus' resurrection. Christ the abandoned, the alone, through his loving obedience, remained in union with his Father. So what seems their moment of greatest separation is, in fact, their moment of greatest union. For the Father's love continues to hand his Son over, and the Son's love continues to surrender. This loving union is more powerful than sin and death. From the isolation of the cross comes the new communion of life in Christ's Spirit.

This mystery of separation and union has great spiritual significance for believers. If Christ was abandoned and died alone, we who believe in him are saved precisely from this fate; we are never ultimately alone. We are always in union with Christ. As Paul says, "Whether we live, or whether we die, we are the Lord's" (Romans 14:8).

Hans Urs von Balthasar (1905–1988), contemporary Swiss theologian noted for his reflections on the death of Christ, has spoken of the Easter mysteries as comprising a drama in three acts: Good Friday, Holy, Saturday, and Easter Sunday. Good Friday represents Christ's active self-surrender;

Holy Saturday is the day of the "descent," the day of silence, the day of Sheol, the day on which Christ lies lifeless in the tomb; and Easter is the day of triumph, the Father's day, the day when the Father shows his power over sin and death by raising the Son to eternal life.

...and on the third day he rose again from the dead

This affirmation, in the middle of the Creed, is the center of faith and is the original nucleus of the first proclamation of the church. Although for us modern Christians, we are apt to think of Jesus primarily as God's Incarnate Son, the church's original proclamation focused on Christ's being raised from the dead. The simple proclamation, of course, later expanded to include profound reflections upon his death on the cross, his ministry of teaching and healing, and his divine origin.

One of the earliest confessions of faith, which centers on the resurrection, is found in Paul's first letter to the Corinthians: "For I delivered to you as of first importance what I also received, that Christ died for our sins in accordance with the scriptures, that he was buried, that he was raised on the third day in accordance with the scriptures, and that he appeared to Cephas, then to the twelve. Then he appeared to more than five hundred brethren at one time, most of whom are still alive, though some have fallen asleep. Then he appeared to James, then to all the apostles. Last of all, as to one untimely born, he appeared also to me" (15: 3–8). Here is the fundamental affirmation of faith. Christ is raised. By whom? Obviously by the God of Israel, the God he called *Abba*.

We also find the phrase in the New Testament that "Jesus rose from the dead" (see Mark 16:9, Acts 10:41, and 1 Corinthians 15:3). At times the Scriptures indicate that the resurrection is the action of God the Father. At other times Jesus, the Son, is seen as the active one. Yet, there is no contradiction here, for whatever Jesus has, is, or does originates from the Father. In his work titled *Mysterium Paschale*, Balthasar indicates the dialectal tension between "was raised" and "rose" when he writes, "If at the extreme obedience of the Son, it was fitting that he allowed himself to be raised by the Father, in no less a way, it belongs to the fulfillment of this obedience, that he allows himself to be given by the Father to 'have life in himself' (Jn. 5:26)."

John's Gospel indicates that through his being resurrected by the Father, Jesus possesses in himself the gift of eternal life. In the famous words of John 11, Jesus says, "I am the resurrection and the life; he who believes in me, though he die, yet shall he live, and whoever lives and believes in me, shall never die" (25–26). If we believe in Jesus, we have the life that will never end, the life that even death cannot destroy. This is why the same Gospel proclaims, "I have come that they may have life and have it abundantly" (John 10:10).

If we think about it, the term *resurrection* is based on a metaphor—the metaphor of lying down to sleep and awakening and getting up. But what lies behind this metaphor of resurrection? Perhaps the most important danger to avoid is thinking of Jesus' resurrection as a return to this life. It's not as if Jesus stood up from his coffin and resumed everyday life. Perhaps we think of rising from the dead in this way, but this is much too trivial an understanding. Lazarus's resurrection apparently was like this—but then Lazarus would have to die again. No. The language of resurrection wants to indicate that Jesus is alive in eternal glory. He is no longer with us in the ordinary way of everyday living. He is in a glorified state; he now dwells in the eternal splendor of the Father. We get some idea of this from the fact that when Jesus appears to his disciples, his coming is always mysterious. He arrives suddenly, passes through doors, the disciples fail to recognize him, and suddenly he is no longer there. All these details indicate a totally new manner of Jesus' being after death.

The passage from 1 Corinthians 15 indicates that the resurrection appearances are central to the New Testament faith in Jesus' resurrection. It is significant that the disciples seem to be totally unprepared for this event. They are hidden away for fear in the upper room. Even when Jesus appears, they are at first skeptical, as we see in the case of Thomas. Mark expresses this point of view when he says that they did not understand the Lord's words that he must rise from the dead (see 9:10). And Luke indicates that Jesus had to explain the Scriptures about himself to his disciples (see 24:27).

Scholars have debated the nature of these appearance events and much has been written about them. In general, we should not understand them as if they were this-worldly historical events that could be recorded by a TV camera. This must be true if people like Mary Magdalene and the disciples on the road to Emmaus fail to recognize him. Rather, it would seem that the Gospels are trying to articulate a mysterious presence of Jesus that the disciples come to through faith. There is no instance of an appearance, for example, in which the one who encounters Jesus refuses to believe. So the Gospels are speaking of faith encounters, unique to be sure, but also shrouded in mystery. We might be inclined to call them *visions,* but even that term is a metaphor. Paul, for example, on the road to Damascus, is knocked to the ground, sees a light, and hears a voice. But this appearance isn't exactly a vision. One theologian has described the appearances as "believing seeing" and "seeing believing."

Another aspect of the New Testament faith in the resurrection is the empty tomb. This is a solid New Testament tradition, although many scholars believe it is not as old as the tradition about the appearances. It is not mentioned, for example, in the passage cited above from 1 Corinthians 15. Although in the Jewish perspective there was no idea of immortality of the soul, there was a hope among large sections of Jews for a resurrection of the dead on the last day. Thus if Jesus' body had remained in the tomb, if it had corrupted, if people could have pointed to the tomb with the body in it, it would have been impossible for the proclamation of the early church to have had credibility. It seems reasonable, therefore, to accept this tradition.

Scholars point out, however, that an empty tomb by itself does not lead to faith in the resurrection. As some gospel stories indicate, there were rumors that the body had been stolen (see Matthew 28: 13–15). So the real solid rock upon which resurrection faith is founded is the ancient tradition that the Lord Jesus manifests himself to various disciples after his death. Thus we could say that the empty tomb is a necessary but not sufficient condition for credibility in Christ's resurrection.

Why do we believe in Christ's resurrection? As we saw from the first article of the Creed, faith is always a free gift made possible by God's grace. Although we can make good arguments based on the testimony of the apostles to show that resurrection faith is reasonable, such arguments cannot coerce a person into believing. A person's freedom is always involved. We bring the entirety of our personal life, with the depths of our human hopes, before the decision to believe in Jesus as eternal life. These influence our openness to faith.

At this point, however, Karl Rahner introduces a beautiful consideration. He has insisted that the world is permeated with God's grace. God wishes everyone to be saved and so God is working mysteriously in each of us, individually, to bring us to salvation. According to Rahner, part of the mystery of grace is the "hope" dimension of life. We all long for life and, we might argue, we all long for a life that the grave cannot rob. Every culture has protested against death as the final word about human life. We invincibly go on hoping, but as human beings we do not have the answer to death. Balthasar says that we are at best like men and women pounding on the door of the underworld begging for a solution. Fortunately, this human search can be seen as guided by God's grace. So we bring all our human longings and desires for life to the good news of the church that Christ has been raised from the dead. In the gospel of the resurrection, we find at last, unexpectedly, the answer to our deepest hopes about life and death. In this sense, too, grace is the final word in coming to faith in the risen Jesus.

He ascended into heaven and is seated at the right hand of the Father

This affirmation of the Creed focuses our attention on our Lord's ascension into heaven; the previous article addressed the resurrection. When we think about it, the language of resurrection and ascension is based on images or metaphors. Resurrection is based on the image of rising from sleep; ascension is based on the image of being lifted up.

In our own day the ascension can cause problems for believers precisely because of the image of being lifted up. We are accustomed to ascending space shuttles, but we are not accustomed to human beings ascending into the heavens and disappearing from sight, as the Acts of the Apostles portrays the ascension of Jesus.

What the metaphor of the ascension points to is Jesus' being glorified with his heavenly Father. He now lives in the eternal splendor or radiance of the Father. The risen glory that is his is promised also to us, his disciples, if we believe in him.

We also note another image: "seated at the right hand of the Father." This, too, is a pictorial way of speaking of Jesus' glorification with his God. It is based on the Old Testament image from the Book of Daniel, where the prophet sees one like a Son of Man seated at the right hand of the Ancient of Days (see Daniel 7:13ff). In the Old Testament the Son of Man was expected to return at the end of time to participate in the final judgment. These ideas were applied to Jesus after his resurrection. Seated at the right hand of God, the Lord Jesus will return to judge humankind on the last day. As John puts it: "The Father has given all judgment to the Son" (5:22).

The idea of Jesus' glorification is common to many New Testament writers, but it is especially Luke who narrates the story of the ascension—which takes place forty days after the resurrection. In the Bible, the number forty is symbolic, representing a certain period, also indicating a certain fullness. The Jews, for example, wander forty years in the desert after their liberation from Egypt. Jesus spends forty days in the desert and is tempted after his baptism. According to Luke, the period of the resurrection appearances lasts forty days and, afterwards, Jesus ascends into heaven.

Luke wants to mark a closure to Jesus' earthly activity. Luke sees three distinctive periods in salvation history: the time of anticipation of the Messiah in the Old Testament; the time of Jesus' earthly ministry; and the time of the church that began on the first Pentecost, the day on which the Holy Spirit descended upon the disciples of Jesus fifty days after the resurrection. The forty days after the resurrection and the fifty-day period leading to Pentecost are, for Luke, full of theological significance.

One of the most important aspects of the ascension is that it brings down the curtain on one act of the drama of salvation and opens it on another. Although Jesus has gone away from us in the flesh, he has not deserted us. For with Pentecost he pours out his Spirit upon us. We are not alone; the Spirit of Jesus is with us.

The fourth Gospel, not strictly speaking of an "ascension," makes similar theological affirmations. Jesus tells the disciples that they should not be sorrowful that he is going away. Although this is a strange claim at face value, it does make sense when we realize that Jesus' departure is his return to his Father, where he shares the Father's everlasting glory.

But there are two more reasons why we should not be sorrowful. Not only should we rejoice for Jesus because he has returned to his Father, but we should be glad because Jesus has been vindicated by God. Thus we also have confidence—

and reason to rejoice—because, as the Lord himself says, he goes to prepare a place for us: "In my Father's house there are many mansions. If it were not so, would I have told you that I go to prepare a place for you?" (John 14:2) The preface for the feast of the ascension also speaks in the same way: "Where he has gone, there we too shall be." He will take us with him. The belief about the ascension reminds us that our destiny is in the home of our heavenly Father.

Finally, there is the promise of the Spirit. How can we forget the pregnant words of Jesus: "I will not leave you desolate. I will come to you" (John 14:18)? These words are spoken in the context of the Last Supper. On one level, they point to Jesus' return after his death, in the resurrection. On a deeper level, however, they point to his return in a new and far deeper way in the gift of the Holy Spirit.

I hope I have been able to communicate that the mystery of the ascension is far more than a historical event in some way analogous to the flight of an airplane or the take-off of a space shuttle. The ascension is a profound truth about the mystery of Christ's destiny and ours. In that sense, the feast of the ascension is a glorious celebration of our Christian hope.

He will come to judge the living and the dead

Undoubtedly, judgment is a key concept in the Bible. In the Old Testament, God is portrayed as a God of love who freely enters into covenant with his people. At the same time, God is seen as a jealous God. If God, for his part, is always faithful to his covenant love, he has the right to expect faithfulness from his people. Understandably, then, the infidelity of God's people provokes the divine wrath. The prophets continually recall to the people the coming day of the Lord and bring before their minds the divine judgment. In the ministry of Jesus, however, the day of wrath is turned into a day of mercy. Jesus comes at the final hour of the world with the message of a divine amnesty. Although God's patience has been tested, God still does not give up on his people.

A fundamental dimension of the faith of the early church was the conviction that Christ will come again. The New Testament, in fact, compares Jesus to the Son of Man, an Old Testament figure to whom God the Father gives an important role in the final judgment. We see this figure frequently in the New Testament as well. For example, after the high priest asks Jesus if he is the Christ or the Messiah, Jesus replies, "I am; and you will see the Son of Man sitting at the right hand of Power, and coming with the clouds of heaven" (Mark 14:62).

For the most part, the early church looked forward to Christ's second coming with great hope. Because the early church was a persecuted church, Christ's second coming was seen as the moment of final deliverance. We see Paul encouraging his communities in the face of death, telling them not to give up hope, for death is not the end. Christ will come again: "For the Lord himself will descend from heaven with a cry of command, with the archangel's call, and with the sound of the trumpet of God. And the dead in Christ will rise first; then we who are alive, who are left, shall be caught up together with them in the clouds to meet the Lord in the air; and so we shall always be with the Lord. Therefore comfort one another with these words" (1 Thessalonians 4:16–18).

It should be stressed that the proclamation of the second coming is a word of great hope. In the first instance, it is a message of comfort and encouragement, not of fear. As we read in the letter to the Hebrews, "Just as it is appointed for men to die once, and after that comes judgment, so Christ, having been offered once to bear the sins of many, will appear a second time, not to deal with sin but to save those who are eagerly awaiting him" (9:27–28).

There is another dimension of judgment, however, one that comes into greater relief as the Christian community becomes more established, and that is the possibility of being condemned by Christ himself. We find a classical instance of this in the parable of the last judgment in Matthew 25:31–46, where Christ the judge divides his community into the sheep and the goats at the final judgment. This scene, which has so influenced Christian art, identifies the goats as those who fail to put into practice the teaching of Christ: They fail to feed the hungry, clothe the naked, and visit those in prison. In short, they fail to see Christ in the least of his brethren. A similar parable is that of the wise and foolish virgins (see Matthew 25:1–13). The foolish virgins are those who are condemned for not bringing oil for their vessels. Hence, their lamps go out and they are not prepared to meet the bridegroom. As a result, they are expelled from the wedding feast. In a beautiful commentary on this passage, Saint Augustine says that the oil we need to keep our lamps burning brightly is charity.

Such parables, which are indeed stern warnings to Christians, are an exhortation both to conversion and to the full practice of the Christian life. The goats in Christ's parable are those who fail to see Christ in the poor and suffering. They know the commandments and, one might even surmise, they are willing to keep them, but they do not have eyes to see. Matthew 25 is about the last judgment, but it is also a parable about Christ's presence in the world. We have to be able to see where Christ is, where the demands of justice are to be met.

The second coming of Christ, as a part of the gospel, thus contains a tension. On the one hand, it is the announcement of a great hope. On the other hand, it is a call to action and a warning about the seriousness of life. Our faith must consist not only in words but also in deeds. As long as we live and as long as time continues, we can never fully resolve this tension. The church has never taught that Christ condemns anyone to hell. The church does proclaim, however, that hell is a real possibility for human beings. It is not for us to try to create some speculative solution to this problem. Rather, with great confidence in the love of Christ, who died for us, we continue to look to him in trust, hoping he will bring us to final redemption. The scales of justice have been tipped in our favor. Meanwhile, we try to put his love into action in our everyday lives, seeing Christ in those whom the Lord puts in our path, especially in the least of his brethren.

I believe in the Holy Spirit

The third article in the Creed is notoriously difficult. We know Jesus from his history among us, and the concept of *Abba* at least aids our imagination in thinking of the God of Jesus. But the Spirit is faceless for many Christians. We are often like the disciples at Ephesus who, when asked if they have received the Spirit, reply that they do not know there is a Holy Spirit (see Acts 19: 1–7).

Both the New Testament and the Old Testament are filled with references to the Spirit, giving us abundant images for God as Spirit. Yet, the Bible is singularly unsystematic in regard to the Spirit. Even in the history of the church, the Holy Spirit has often been neglected. The Spirit certainly has come into play at certain moments of church history: in periods of extreme fervor and enthusiasm and at turning points in history that often witnessed to new outpourings of the Spirit. At the beginning of the second millennium, for example, Joachim of Fiore (1132–1202), an Italian abbot, thought that the third age of the world was dawning. He saw the Old Testament as the time of the Father, the first millennium as the time of the Son, and the new millennium as being the third age, that of the Spirit. At our own moment of history, as we enter the early years of a new millennium, it ought not to surprise us to find expectations about the last days, fears of the end of the world, and new manifestations of the Spirit that call for careful discernment.

When controversies broke out in the early centuries of the church, they were usually about the nature and person of Christ. In the fourth century, for example, the burning question was whether the Eternal Word of God, as John describes Jesus (see 1:1), was really equal to the Father or was it merely an intermediary between God and humanity. The underlying question was really whether God could come into full contact with the world through the Incarnation.

When the the Council of Nicea settled this question in the affirmative in 325, with the declaration that the Logos was fully equal to the Father, it was natural for the next question to be about the Holy Spirit. Fifty years after Nicea, therefore, another council was held at Constantinople, and the following words were added to the Creed: "I believe in the Holy Spirit, the Lord and giver of life, who proceeds from the Father, and with the Father and the Son is worshiped and glorified, and who spoke through the prophets." Each of these words was carefully chosen. The council called the Spirit "Lord" or *Kyrios*, the same title that was given to Jesus to express his divinity. The Spirit "gives life," a reference to the role of sanctification that the Spirit fulfills in baptism, which gives the neophyte—the newly baptized person—eternal life.

Then there are the two critical words: "worshiped" and "glorified." Only God is worthy of worship so here, too, we have an implicit reference to the divinity of the Spirit. Thus we can say that by the year 381, the year of the Council of Constantinople, the church had fully affirmed her faith in the divinity of the Holy Spirit and proclaimed the Spirit to be the third Person of the Holy Trinity, co-equal with the Father and the Son.

With this foundation in place, subsequent centuries explored the depths of the reality of the Spirit in the life of God and in the history of salvation. Let us all too briefly suggest a few of the salient points of these developments.

How can we, for example, conceive of the role of the Holy Spirit in the Trinity? First, we should note that theology has always given a priority to the place of the Father in the Trinity. The Father is the source of everything in God. The Father, in an eternal act of love, begets the Son. The Son is both the Father's perfect self-expression as well as the Father's perfect self-gift. The Father wants to hold nothing back but gives everything to the Son. It was Saint Augustine who beautifully suggested that the Spirit is the bond of love in the Trinity. As far back as the first letter of John, we learn that God is love. But if the whole Trinity is love, we can say that the Spirit is love in person. The Spirit is the bond of love between the Father and the Son. The Trinity can thus be seen as the perfect community, not a community made up of three separate individuals but three Persons who nonetheless are only one God. In the words of the preface for Trinity Sunday: "…three Persons equal in majesty, undivided in splendor, yet one Lord, one God, ever to be adored in your everlasting glory."

Within the Trinity we can also see the Spirit as pure gift. The Spirit receives everything from the Father and the Son. The Spirit is pure receptivity. But as the Spirit receives all, the Spirit is also the possibility of God's being gift to the world. God does not keep his love for himself but rather, offers an openness to the world in the Spirit. Just as the Spirit is communion in the Trinity, so the Spirit makes possible our communion with God.

If the Spirit is the bond of union in the Trinity, the Spirit also continually unites Jesus to the Father. Jesus is filled with the fullness of the Spirit from the moment of his conception. At baptism he receives a new outpouring of the Spirit to undertake his mission. Immediately afterwards, he is led into the desert by the Spirit and there he is tempted but remains faithful to his filial vocation. Later, during his ministry, he preaches prophetically in the power of the Spirit. Then, at the moment of death, as John tells us, Jesus hands over his Spirit and, on Easter night, he breathes on the apostles and bestows the gift of his Spirit on them (see 20:22).

So Jesus, in his entire being and in all his activity, is full of the Spirit. He is always in union with his Father for the Spirit of the Father dwells in him. The Spirit's role is to unite Father and Son, not only in the Trinity but in the ministry of Jesus.

Finally, we come to the role of the Holy Spirit today. Perhaps most importantly the Holy Spirit is Christ's gift to us believers. Although Christ has ascended into heaven, he has not really departed from us. He has come to us in a new way through the Spirit. In John's Gospel, Jesus says that he and his Father "will come to him and make our home with him" (14:23). Jesus is truly dwelling within us by the gift of the Holy Spirit, whom we have received in baptism. Because we have God's Spirit dwelling within us, we share Christ's own life, what the Greek Fathers of the church called *divinization*. Again it is John who so beautifully underscores this fact by offering us the Lord's famous metaphor of the vine and the branches. In that metaphor, Jesus invites us to abide in him. We should be grafted onto him like the branches to the vine— and this grafting is the work of Christ's Spirit (see John 15).

The Spirit unites each disciple with Christ. The Spirit is also at work in the church, uniting disciples to one another, each Christian having his or her own uniqueness and his or her own gifts. Paul stresses, however, that although there are many gifts, there is only one Spirit (see 1 Corinthians 12:4–7).

The Spirit of peace, harmony, and charity is the bond of unity in the Christian community.

The New Testament contains abundant passages about the mission of the Spirit. Paul, for example, has a lot to say about the gifts of the Spirit, about the liberty that the Spirit brings, and about the fruits that follow from the divine indwelling. And John offers us the moving metaphor of the Paraclete—a word that indicates an "attorney." Just as the attorney pleads the case of his or her client, so the Holy Spirit pleads our case with the Father—just as Jesus pleaded our case during his earthly ministry. The Paraclete also defends us against the spirit of the world—all that resists Jesus. The world, in John's sense, will seek to do to us what it did to Jesus, but the Spirit of Jesus will defend us in our time of need.

According to John's Gospel, the Spirit is also our consoler. The Spirit consoles us with the presence of the risen Jesus, helps us remember Jesus, and enlightens our minds to understand the meaning of Jesus for our lives here and now. The church has continued to ponder the mystery of Jesus over the centuries—over the millennia. It is the Spirit who helps us ponder, understand, and apply the message of Jesus to our historical situation.

The Bible has a host of images that evoke for us the meaning of the Spirit. Often the word *spirit* is linked to "breath"; the Pentecost story associates the Spirit with wind, the mighty force of God's presence in the world (see Acts 2:1–2); and John thinks of the Spirit as our teacher (see 14:26). Finally, we might mention the image of fire. Luke says that Christ will baptize with fire and the Spirit (see 3:16). Again, we refer to the Pentecost story and see how it associates the coming of the Spirit with tongues of fire. In this sense, the Spirit is the one who ignites us with the love of God, the divine love that burns within us. This love is a powerful force in our lives, but it is not just an individual possession. Rather, the burning presence of the Spirit also drives us out in mission, to bear witness to Christ, and to proclaim God's love to the world—to those we meet in family, friendship, and work.

...the holy catholic Church

Today, in a church fraught with many tensions, it is easy to think of the church in purely political categories, emphasizing the many issues about which Catholics disagree. But these things do not bring us to the heart of the church. From the perspective of faith, the church is part of the mystery of salvation. The church is where Christ is to be found in a privileged way. We could even say that God destines all men and women to be part of the church insofar as he destines all of us to Christ. In coming to Christ we cannot by-pass his church.

Although the Bible offers a host of images that speak of the church, three central images of the church refer to the Trinity. First, the church is the work of the Father, since the Father elects us to be his new people. If, in the Old Testament, God makes a covenant with Israel, in the New Testament he chooses us to be the people of the new covenant. This image is beautifully expressed in 1 Peter: "You are a chosen race, a royal priesthood, a holy nation, God's own people, that you may declare the wonderful deeds of him who called you out of darkness into his marvelous light. Once you were no people but now you are God's people; once you had not received mercy but now you have received mercy" (2:9–10).

Second, the church is the work of Christ. Paul develops a beautiful Christ-focused image of the church. He tells us that we are the body of Christ—Christ is the head and we are the members: "Just as the body is one and has many members, and all the members of the body, though many, are one body, so it is with Christ. For by one Spirit we were all baptized into one body—Jews or Greeks, slaves or free—and all were made to drink of one Spirit" (1 Corinthians 12:12–13). The letter to the Ephesians offers another strong Christ-focused image: the church as the spouse of Christ. Christ is the bridegroom and we, the church, are his spouse.

These two images complement each other. The image of the body is an organic one. We are incorporated into Christ so that, in one sense, we can say that we are Christ. Saint Augustine frequently stressed this depth of our unity with Christ; he spoke of the church as the "total Christ." But this image alone would not do justice to the full reality of the church, for we are also sinful. We are not simply the same as Christ. Thus the image of the bride stresses the distinction between Christ and the church. We must grow into the spotless bride of Christ.

Third, the church is the work of the Spirit. For example, Paul calls the church the temple of the Holy Spirit: "Do you not know that you are God's temple and that God's Spirit dwells in you?" (1 Corinthians 3:16) In other words, individual Christians bear the Spirit within themselves—as does the community. John says that in the new messianic era, we are to worship in Spirit and in truth. The Christian community has replaced the Temple of Jerusalem and the church is now God's temple, filled with the powerful presence of the Holy Spirit.

These three images attest to the trinitarian dimension of the church. There are, of course, many other important images that highlight different aspects of the mystery. For example, Saint Ignatius Loyola (1491–1556), founder of the Jesuits, mystic, and author of the *Spiritual Exercises*, offered an image that is not only one of my favorites but also has sound biblical roots: the church as the Lord's vineyard. Isaiah, for example, speaks of Israel as the Lord's vineyard (see 5:7); the psalmist prays that the Lord will not fail to cultivate his holy vine (see Psalms 80:14–15); and Mark develops the parable of the tenants of the Lord's vineyard (see 12:1–11). For Ignatius, this image offered an apostolic appeal. Recognizing that there is so much work to be done to cultivate the Lord's vineyard, Ignatius wanted the Society of Jesus to be made up of workers ready to be sent to any part of the Lord's vineyard to bear apostolic fruit.

In contemporary theology, many reflections have been offered to illumine the nature of the church. Avery Dulles, a contemporary Jesuit theologian, and Karl Rahner suggest that we think of the church as the sacrament of Christ in the world. The key here is Jesus' words, "He who has seen me has seen the Father" (John 14:9). Jesus makes the reality of God visible in the world through his person and ministry. In Jesus we see who God is and who God wants to be for us, namely a God dedicated to human beings, a God laboring so that we might realize our full humanity. By becoming his church, we, in turn, become the sacrament of salvation for the world. We carry on the mission of Jesus, living as he lived and so making the splendor of God visible for all to see.

This is an exalted vision of the church, one that the church often fails to realize. But this vision sets the ideal for which we are to strive. In John's words, we are to become one in Christ, one with our Savior, and one with one another, "so that the world may believe" (17:21). The great document of the Second Vatican Council on the church (*Dogmatic Constitution on the Church*) begins with the words, "Christ is the light of all nations." When the church realizes her true vocation she does, indeed, become a light shining in the dark.

Dulles also proposes a simple definition of the church as the community of disciples. What brings us together as church is the call that each of us has felt to be a disciple of Jesus, a call initiated by Jesus, summoning us to follow him. It is the Lord who calls us into fellowship. As disciples, we represent Christ by being his messengers. We bear the good news of Jesus to others. Jesus is also present to us in the midst of the community of his disciples, especially by feeding us with his Word and his body and blood. Christ's presence in the community of disciples is dynamic as he transforms the life of his disciples by summoning them to imitate him by serving one another.

But what can we say about the mission of this holy Catholic Church? Why does it exist? First, the church exists to preach the good news of Jesus to the world. An immediate consequence of the resurrection of Jesus was the *kerygma*, that is, the proclamation of what God has done in Jesus. The first apostles boldly proclaimed, "We cannot but speak of what we have seen and heard" (Acts 4:20)—and the church continues this task through the ages. The church must, therefore, always be related to the world beyond itself. It does not exist for its own sake but for the salvation of the world.

Second, the church is a community of action. As Saint Ignatius Loyola says, "Love manifests itself in deeds." As a community of disciples that seeks to do what Jesus did, the church represents in our world the type of activity the Lord Jesus requires of his followers. These actions are of two types. First, the community seeks to create signs of hope for the world. One of the greatest of these signs, of course, is the Christian family—often referred to as the "domestic church." Second, the community seeks to create movements of resistance against evil—thus the whole history of charitable works, hospitals, orphanages, and works of education. Contemporary examples would be the church's solidarity with victims of injustice: women, the elderly, the unborn, the victims of racism, and those who suffer with AIDS. Although the church in the contemporary world has become a much greater voice for justice, much more needs to be done to make its proclamation of the good news credible.

Finally, the church is the home of believers. To feel at home is one of the great gifts of being human: to be in a place where we are accepted, where we do not feel alienated. The church is called to be God's house where God's children feel at home, accepted for who they are, with their limitations, failings, and sinfulness. Christians are continually grateful for this home, finding there, among other things, the daily nourishment of God's Word. The Bible is an infinite treasure of the church offered to us each day for our nourishment. In the church—as God's house—we also find guidance through the teaching office and pastoral care of the ordained and other lay ministers. And most important of all, the church offers us the daily Bread of Life, the Eucharist, which is food for our journey until we finally arrive at our heavenly home at the end of life's pilgrimage.

The Jesuit Urban Center in Boston welcomes the gay and lesbian community living in the area. It has a ministry of outreach to those affected by HIV and those suffering from AIDS. Many of these persons who have felt rejected by the church are finding a home where they experience God's love. The Catholic cathedral nearby has built up a ministry to the Hispanic community that suffers from poverty and alienation. People are made to feel welcomed and accepted by this ministry. Saint Aloysius, the Jesuit church in Washington, D.C., has a social center that provides daily meals for the hungry. These are simply a few examples of God's welcome extended to those living on the margins. These ministries nurture all with God's love, which is proclaimed in his Word and in the offer of the Eucharist.

...the communion of saints

By our baptism, we are all holy. We were filled with God's own life when we were washed in the waters of baptism. Thus it is not surprising that Paul often addresses his communities as saints: "Paul, called by the will God to be an apostle of Christ Jesus, and our brother Sosthenes, to the Church of God which is at Corinth, to those sanctified in Christ Jesus, called to be saints together with all those who in every place call on the name of our Lord Jesus Christ" (1 Corinthians 1:1–2). Holiness is, therefore, the vocation of all disciples. As Jesus himself said in the Sermon on the Mount, "You must be perfect as your heavenly Father is perfect" (Matthew 5:48).

When we look at the history of Christianity, however, we see that the vocation to holiness has caused profound theological debates and has often provoked anxiety in the heart of believers. It is important to recognize that God is the one who takes the initiative in the Christian life. We are totally dependent on God for everything. Whatever we do is a response to grace. All of us, ultimately, live by God's forgiveness that we receive from Christ in our baptism. We have absolutely nothing that we can call our own. Everything is grace.

The Catholic tradition has always stressed the priority of grace. Martin Luther (1483–1546), Protestant reformer of the sixteenth century, coined the famous phrase *grace alone,* meaning that we are saved sheerly by grace without the need for good works. Catholic theology, of course, rejected this teaching and emphasized that we cannot dispense with good works. Grace calls forth a response. Theologian Dietrich Bonhoeffer warned against what he called *cheap grace*, grace that does not require anything. In fairness to Luther, he recognized this truth. For him, good works would flow from faith like good fruit from a healthy tree.

So we have to live with a subtle but important tension: We must be receptive to God's grace, forgiveness, and reconciling work in our lives, but we must also be responsive. Grace must find an active, responsive chord in our hearts that expresses itself in good works and deeds of love.

As we have seen, this third article of the Creed stresses the solidarity that binds together all of Christ's faithful. The church on earth is the communion of saints, the living fellowship of all those who have been sanctified by Christ's death. But the church on earth reaches beyond time and space. Our fellowship is also with the saints in heaven, those who presently enjoy God's presence. This same communion also embraces those who are dead and are still being purified, a state that is called *purgatory*. We actually know very little about purgatory but since God is love, we do know that we can only see God face to face when our hearts are fully purified.

In the Catholic tradition there are at least two important truths about the communion of saints. First, we are bound together by mutual prayer and intercession. Those of us here on earth can pray for one another and we can pray for the souls in purgatory. Even more important, the saints in heaven intercede for us—in fact, a mark of the holiness of the saints is their desire to intercede for us. They don't want to enjoy heaven for themselves alone. Rather, they feel bound to us and want to bring us with them into the kingdom. A beautiful example of this comes from the life of Thérèse of Lisieux (1873–1897), a Carmelite nun who was declared a doctor (an outstanding teacher) of the church by Pope John Paul II. Before she died, Thérèse, popularly known as the Little Flower, pledged that she would spend her heaven interceding for sinners. Our greatest intercessor, of course, is Mary, the Mother of the Church, who guides and helps us with a mother's love.

The second aspect of the communion of saints is the fellowship of suffering. As Paul says, no one lives or dies merely for himself (see Romans 14:7). Hence, even our suffering can be mutually beneficial. The grace we receive now, for example, may come from the sufferings of a Christian we do not know in this life. Likewise, we can offer our own suffering for other members of Christ's Body. Solidarity in suffering is one of the great consolations of Christian faith. No

Christian is alone in the last analysis. The risen Christ is with us, as are all the saints with their prayers and sufferings.

Only in heaven will Christ's church be the "Bride without spot or wrinkle" (Ephesians 5:27). Here below, we remain a mixture of saints and sinners. The Catholic tradition is very realistic about this: We are, indeed, called to holiness but, at any given moment in history, the church is a great mixture of saints and sinners. However, the grace of the holiest aids sinners in their weakness. As Matthew's Gospel attests, the church here on earth is like a vast field made up of wheat and darnel, and the final separation will take place only at the last judgment (see 13:24–30). This vision can give us a healthy realism about the church, but it should also inspire us to go about our work humbly, doing what we can to make Christ's church on earth the communion of saints that it is called to be.

...the forgiveness of sins

The message of divine forgiveness is at the heart of the New Testament and of the ministry of Jesus. This should not be seen primarily as the offer of individual forgiveness but rather as the forgiveness of God's people. Although the notion of the free covenant that God makes with Israel is at the heart of the

Old Testament, a constant Old Testament motif is Israel's infidelity. The prophets keep calling Israel back to fidelity to the God of the covenant and, indeed, there is the threat that Israel could so try God's patience as to lead God to forsake the covenant.

This is the context for understanding the ministry of Jesus. He is God's final prophet, the Son who comes to woo Israel back to the divine love. He stands at the end of the ages with a message of God's final offer of forgiveness—and the time is short. So Jesus says, "Repent and believe the good news" (Mark 1:15). The good news is precisely God's offer of reconciliation, which explains many aspects of the ministry of Jesus, such as his association with tax collectors and prostitutes. These social outcasts become symbols for what God is offering to his people—reconciliation. What's more, these people accept the Lord's offer, whereas the religious leaders harden their hearts against Jesus.

As the ambassador of divine mercy, Jesus seeks to incarnate God's forgiveness in his ministry of preaching and in his deeds, which express God's loving outreach to sinners. A beautiful example of this ministry of forgiveness is found toward the beginning of Mark's Gospel, when stretcher bearers lower a man who is paralyzed through the roof of a building so that he might reach Jesus. When Jesus beholds the man and his plight, his first words are, "My son, your sins are forgiven." When Jesus is challenged by the scribes as to his power and right to forgive sins, he heals the man's physical infirmity and offers that as a sign of his divine authority. "But that you may know that the Son of Man has authority on earth to forgive sins, I say to you, rise, take up your pallet and go home" (see Mark 2:1–12).

The subsequent rejection of Jesus by the religious authorities, then, becomes one of the key elements leading to his death; Israel rejects her Messiah. Is this, therefore, a definite break on God's part with the covenant? Have the limits of God's forgiveness finally been reached? Writers like Paul, meditating on this, offer the conviction that God uses the death of Jesus not as a definitive rejection but as an opening of his love to the pagans as well. According to Paul, even Jesus' death does not lead God to reject Israel. The chosen people will be brought back to the God of the covenant after the conversion of the pagan nations of the world.

One of the great insights of the early Christian community is that Jesus' death is the extension of God's forgiveness to all. We find this conviction, for example, in Paul's letter to the Romans: "While we were yet helpless, at the right time Christ died for the ungodly. Why, one will hardly die for a righteous man—though perhaps for a good man one will dare even to die. But God shows his love for us in that while we were yet sinners Christ died for us" (5:6–7). The first letter of Peter speaks in a similar vein: "For Christ also died for sins once for all, the righteous for the unrighteous, that he might bring us to God" (3:18).

Christ's death and resurrection, therefore, means the offer of God's forgiveness for those who believe in him, and the process by which we enter into this forgiveness is faith in Jesus. For adult converts, this faith is made visible in the waters of baptism. Baptism is *par excellence* the sacrament of the divine forgiveness and mercy. When the New Testament mentions these mysteries, it is within the context of adults who go through a process of conversion—a movement from sin and selfishness to faith and new life in Christ. The culmination of this process of conversion is the sacrament of baptism. In the waters of baptism our sins are washed away; we are made new. As a symbol of this purity, the newly baptized are given white garments. In Paul's typically succinct words, "The old has passed away, behold, the new has come" (2 Corinthians 5:17).

The early Christian community thought of only one sacrament of forgiveness: baptism. Later, however, the church had to face the question of how to deal with baptized Christians who denied their faith after baptism, or who fell into other grave sins such as murder or adultery. Gradual reflection led the church to understand that it could, in fact, offer forgiveness for even these grave sins. This took place through public penance and reconciliation on Holy Thursday.

In the course of centuries, the practice of individual confession developed, in which baptized Christians could receive sacramental absolution for their sins. Confession has become the sacrament to which Christians bring their grave sins, appealing to the divine mercy, and their lesser sins, asking the Lord's pardon and healing as they seek to lead a more authentic Christian life.

The church actually celebrates the reality of God's forgiveness in all its sacraments and in its pastoral efforts to bring about reconciliation wherever there is alienation, oppression, and injustice in the world. These actions spring from the experience of having received forgiveness from Jesus, especially in his death and resurrection. Reconciliation is at the heart of the Christian life. As Paul puts it, "God was in Christ reconciling the world to himself, not counting their trespasses against them, and entrusting to us the message of reconciliation" (2 Corinthians 5:19).

...the resurrection of the body and life everlasting

As we saw earlier, the heart of Christian faith is belief in Christ's resurrection. Here, at the end of the Creed, we affirm our hope that we, too, will one day share in that resurrection. Where he is, we too shall be.

It is impossible to conceive the manner of this resurrection, of course, or what our risen bodies will be like. Even in the New Testament, Paul recognizes this. He speaks of a spiritual body: "What is sown is perishable, what is raised is imperishable. It is sown in dishonor, it is raised in glory. It is sown in weakness, it is raised in power. It is sown a physical body, it is raised a spiritual body" (1 Corinthians 15:42–44). Again, this is a very general idea that intends to express the fact that our bodies will be transformed. Christian faith does not profess belief in an immortality of the soul alone. Rather, the full human being—body and soul—will be redeemed in its totality.

Although it is impossible to describe the risen body, certain theologians have offered their reflections. For example, Sandra Schneiders, Catholic biblical scholar and feminist theological, makes a number of interesting points about the glorified body. According to her analysis, the resurrection of the body means at least three things. First, we will be the same persons we have always been. Second, our bodies will continue to distinguish us from others. Third, our bodies will make possible our interaction with others and will be the source of a network of relations with others. This last point is important for what we have already learned about the communion of saints.

These points become clearer if we think of them in relation to Jesus. After his resurrection, though glorified, Jesus is still recognized by his disciples. In fact, the disciples can distinguish Jesus from other people. Jesus is able to interact with his disciples by revealing himself to them—and through faith, they continued to be in relationship with him.

Our body is our means of being in the world. In other words, we are present in the world and we are present to others through our body—"body" in the broadest sense of the word (not just a physical lump of chemicals but as a real presence, including gestures and language). One difference between a corpse and a body is that a corpse is not fully present in the world; the network of relationships has been broken. But with the resurrection of the body, the full extent of our relationships will be restored: our relationship with God, others, and the cosmos.

Through our bodies, here and now, we are part of the cosmos, and we celebrate the reality of the cosmos every day through work and play, sport and art, poetry and dance. And of course friendship and love are celebrated through the body. The belief in the resurrection of the body affirms the fact that all of these bodily realities, so beautiful in themselves, will not disappear but are destined to last in the kingdom of God. Commenting upon the *Divine Comedy* by Dante Alighieri (1265–1321), the father of Italian literature, Balthasar notes that Beatrice's presence in paradise is of great importance to the Christian tradition, for she reminds us that the Lord will redeem our earthly loves. We do not lose the beloved in heaven; rather, we bring all our earthly loves with us.

The Creed ends with the words "life everlasting." Of course these words refer to the eternal life we will share with God in his kingdom. We should not forget, however, that eternal life begins here and now. John stresses this truth *par excellence*. The Lord Jesus tells us, "I am the resurrection and the life" (11:25). By believing in him, by welcoming his Word, and by receiving his body and blood in the Eucharist, we already share in eternal life. By our baptism we have the divine life pulsating within us. So what will happen to us after death and on the last day is really a continuation of what has already begun. To quote Balthasar once again, only a thin veil separates us from eternity. In death the veil will be removed and we will come into the full possession of the eternal life which we have already received.

Questions for Reflection: *How does the Creed fashion your life as a Catholic Christian? How might you use the Creed to explain your beliefs as a Catholic to your non-believing friends? How is the Creed a summary of the entire gospel of Jesus Christ? Can the study of the Creed help you in your life of prayer?*

Chapter 2

The Seven Sacraments

Baptism
Confirmation
Eucharist
Reconciliation

Anointing of the sick
Holy orders
Marriage

The sacraments are signs of Christ, the word *sign* being used in the deepest sense of the word, not in some arbitrary sense. For example, although the red traffic light signifies "stop," any color could have been chosen as long as everyone agreed to it. I've often had the experience of stopping at a red light and wondering why I should wait when no cars are approaching the intersection. Surely the traffic signal is something arbitrary—an indication—"pointing" toward what I *should do*. Other signs, however, express the reality to which they point—a kiss, for example. When spouses kiss, they are expressing the deep reality of their affection and commitment. We spontaneously recognize this truth when we feel repelled by Judas's use of a kiss to betray Jesus (see Matthew 26:48–49).

The Christian sacraments are signs in this deeper sense. They are human realities—words and gestures of our material world—that make Christ present. For example, baptism uses water to signify that the person baptized is cleansed by Christ and is recreated by his love.

What is peculiar about the sacraments is that they are *signs of Christ*. Each one in some way makes Christ present here and now.

Catholic theology has always believed that Christ instituted the sacraments—and, in fact, all the sacraments are rooted in the life of Jesus in some way. The Eucharist, for example, is rooted in his table fellowship with tax collectors and sinners; it is also based on the actions of Jesus at the Last Supper. The anointing of the sick is rooted in Jesus' healing ministry.

Although it is impossible, however, to point to exact moments when Jesus formally instituted each of the sacraments, it is critical for us to understand how these actions of the church have their basis in the life and ministry of Jesus.

Moreover, it is the risen Christ who formally founds the church and its sacraments. Truly, the risen Lord is the basis of all the church's sacramental actions.

The sacraments give grace precisely by being the signs they are. Just as the kiss expresses and deepens the love between two persons so that the act of kissing not only makes that love real but also deepens that love, so too the use of these signs draws the believer more deeply into the life of Christ. Performing the sacramental actions with faith brings with it a fuller participation in Christ. Hence, the sacraments let the eternal life of Christ well up more deeply within us.

The Catholic tradition recognizes seven sacraments, seven signs of Christ that graft us onto him, our vine: baptism, confirmation, and Eucharist (the sacraments of initiation); reconciliation and anointing of the sick (the sacraments of healing); and holy orders and marriage (the sacraments of vocation). We will look at the history and significance of each sacrament individually.

Baptism

One of the most striking words of our Lord is the saying in which he compares his death to baptism: "I have a baptism to be baptized with and how I am constrained until it be accomplished" (Luke 12:50). In this context, baptism is more dramatic than a mere washing. The image of water in baptism is linked to the terrifying and destructive power of water, something like the image we find in Psalm 69: "Save me, O God! For the waters have come up to my neck. I sink in deep mire, where there is no foothold; I have come into deep waters, and the flood sweeps over me" (1–2).

One of the clearest injunctions of the Lord that the apostles remember and pass on is Jesus' command to baptize his followers. Matthew 28 is unambiguous: "Go therefore and make disciples of all nations, baptizing them in the name of the Father, the Son and the Holy Spirit" (19).

From earliest times the church initiated adults by the rite of baptism, a ritual that centered on the baptismal pool. The adult converts entered fully into this font, were submerged in the waters, and emerged to be clothed in a new and pure white vestment. The symbolism of immersion was linked to death. Just as Christ went into the tomb and emerged to new life, so the catechumens—those who had been preparing to become Christians—went into the pool of baptism, were immersed, and then rose to a new Christian existence. Paul captures this symbolism well in the letter to the Romans: "Do you not know that all of us who have been baptized into Christ Jesus were baptized into his death? We were buried therefore with him by baptism into death, so that as Christ was raised from the dead by the glory of the Father, we too might walk in newness of life" (6:3–4).

Baptism, then, refers to the process of dying and rising with Christ. As new converts come to know Christ, they enter into the suffering, death, and resurrection of Jesus. They accept the way of Jesus by turning away from lives of selfishness toward Christ's new pattern of self-giving. They make Jesus' words their own: "If any man would come after me, let him deny himself and take up his cross daily and follow me. For whoever would save his life will lose it; and whoever loses his life for my sake, he will save it" (Luke 9:23–24).

If baptism is conceived as passing through the destructive power of water, symbolizing death in Christ, it is also seen as a cleansing. This cleansing is linked to the process of entering into Christ's discipleship and accepting the mystery of his death and resurrection. The newly baptized is cleansed of all sin. The "old" person dies in baptism, and the "new" person—the new Christian—leads a totally different form of life. Paul expresses this succinctly in the second letter to the Corinthians: "If anyone is in Christ, he is a new creation; the old has passed away, behold, the new has come" (5:17).

Thus far we have spoken of baptism in relation to Christ; baptism is dying and rising with Christ. But we should bring in the Holy Spirit as well. The risen Jesus is present in the world through his Spirit, and this Spirit is given to us in baptism. Through baptism we are filled with the Spirit of God, the Spirit of Jesus. We have the Holy Spirit dwelling within us. This means that we are holy and that we share in the Sonship of Christ. We have that relationship to the Father that Jesus had. Paul says in a moving passage, "God has sent the Spirit of his Son into our hearts crying, 'Abba, Father!'" (Galatians 4:6).

Because we are made holy by the Spirit dwelling within us, we become like God. We resemble his Son and we are pleasing to him. The holiness we have by virtue of our baptism is called *sanctifying grace.* Grace is simply another word for the gift of holiness that comes to us through the Holy Spirit given to us in baptism. This gift is all the more remarkable when we consider the history of sin in the human race.

When looking at the human situation, Paul makes a comparison between Christ and Adam. As we saw in the Creed, the first Adam was created in the image of God, but Adam lost this image by sin. Paul sees Christ as the new Adam who overturns human sin and restores the divine image in men and women. In Romans, Paul writes, "As sin came into the world through one man and death through sin, and so death spread to all men because all men sinned . . . but the free gift is not like the trespass. For if many died through one man's trespass, much more have the grace of God and the free gift in the grace of that one man Jesus Christ abounded for many" (5:12–15).

Paul's thinking was the inspiration for what later theology called *original sin*, and Saint Augustine developed this idea further in the fifth century. Everyone participates in the sin of Adam; we all share in the human situation of guilt. As members of the human race, we are implicated in the sin of Adam. We are born into a world alienated from God. But our solidarity with Christ recreates the image of God in us. God's original plan for the world is restored by Christ's death and resurrection. By participating in Christ's saving mystery through baptism, we are inheritors of eternal life.

The notion of original sin can be misleading, however. Whereas *personal sin* is something we do, original sin expresses the human condition, something we find ourselves "in." This concept expresses a lack: Humankind without Christ is deprived of the divine Sonship that God intends for the human race. Baptism removes this lack; it recreates the fellowship with God that Christ as the divine Son enjoys and makes possible for us. We should always remember, of course, that everything Christ does for us is at the behest of the Father. The Father never stops loving humankind, even after the sin of Adam. It is because of that love, in fact, that the Father sends the Son. As John says, "God so loved the world that he sent his only Son, that whoever believes in him should not perish but have eternal life. For God sent the Son into the world not to condemn the world, but that the world might be saved through him" (3:16–17). In this context we can understand why the Easter hymn proclaimed at the lighting of the Easter candle cries out, "O happy sin of Adam that merited so great a redeemer."

Thus far we have indicated that baptism frees us from sin and gives us the new life of Christ. Baptism also makes us members of the church, incorporating us into God's holy people. Baptism is the welcoming celebration of the adult believer into the Christian community. If the baptized is a child, it is a welcoming of that child, a proclamation of God's love for that child, and an incorporation of the child into Christ. The priest meets the parents and godparents at the doors of the church, welcomes them, and leads them and the child to the font of baptism. Unforgettable are the words of greeting as the priest signs the infant with the cross and declares, "I claim you for Christ."

Welcoming, of course, implies the beginning or the arrival of something. The welcoming ritual of baptism is part of the "initiation" process of a person into the church. Thus the church speaks of the "sacraments of initiation," and baptism is the rite of initiation *par excellence*. Baptism is the gateway to all the other sacraments. What is done in baptism is then confirmed with the sealing of the Holy Spirit. If the newly baptized person is an adult, this takes place immediately in the sacrament of confirmation. In the West, if the newly baptized is a child, confirmation is postponed until the child or young adult can fully "confirm" the decision of faith. The rites of initiation are completed when the newly baptized receives the Eucharist, for in the Eucharist the full fellowship of humanity with God is celebrated. At the eucharistic table we eat the Bread of Life and God's purposes for humanity are fulfilled: We live in God and God lives in us. God has always destined us for this communion. Communion with God is the goal of all God's activity on our behalf and the end toward which all the sacraments are celebrated.

Confirmation

Understanding confirmation today is complicated by difficult pastoral questions about the proper age to receive the sacrament. These questions are the result of a shift in the original place of the sacrament within the rites of initiation. The three sacraments of initiation—baptism, confirmation, and Eucharist—were meant for adult Christians. In the ancient church, those preparing to become Christian were baptized and then anointed with chrism and sealed with the Spirit.

Following that, they received the Eucharist—all this at the Easter vigil. With the emergence of infant baptism, however, the question of the timing of confirmation arose. In the Eastern Church, infants currently receive all three sacraments of initiation at one time. In the West, however, infants receive only baptism; they receive Eucharist years later and then are confirmed, thus disturbing the integrity of the rite of initiation. As a result, confirmation tends to be a kind of puberty rite linked in principle to making an adult commitment to the faith.

But what is the significance of confirmation if the church has always taught that a believer is filled with the Holy Spirit in baptism, and that through the gift of the Holy Spirit, the newly baptized becomes a new creation? One approach is to look at the unity of Christ's suffering, death, and resurrection. The Easter mystery consists of the death and resurrection of Jesus and the sending of the Spirit. Easter is really a fifty-day celebration that culminates on Pentecost. Baptism can be seen as celebrating the aspect of death and resurrection, as being plunged into the death of Jesus to rise to new life. The Holy Spirit, of course, is involved in this, but confirmation emphasizes the Pentecost dimension. The apostles are frightened after the Lord's ascension, and huddle together in the upper room for fear of being arrested, just as Jesus was. The Holy Spirit comes upon them as wind, rests above them as tongues of fire, and gives them courage. As a result, they go out—unafraid—to preach the risen Jesus. So in confirmation, baptized Christians are given the strength of the Holy Spirit for mission. They are fully empowered to be witnesses for Christ. They bind themselves more fully to the church and its mission. They assume their part in the work of carrying on the ministry of Jesus in the world.

In the West this sacrament is called *confirmation*, indicating that it "confirms" what happens in baptism. In the East it is called *chrismation*, indicating the anointing with the Holy Sprit. In either case, the sacrament consists in the laying on of hands by the bishop or the priest and the anointing of the forehead with sacred oil, which is consecrated by the bishop on Holy Thursday at what is called the *chrism mass*. During the moment of anointing, the bishop prays: "Be sealed through the gift of God, the Holy Spirit."

Among the many symbols of confirmation, the sacred chrism is richly symbolic. It recalls the anointing of priests and kings, a rite that is still practiced in modern coronation ceremonies. Oil is used to make the body supple, to prepare it for an athletic contest, for example. It also has medicinal and healing effects. Oil also contains perfume and so indicates the sweet-smelling fragrance that emanates from the transformed life of the Christian who has received the gift of the Holy Spirit. Jesus is called the Christ, the anointed one. He is preeminently anointed since he is our King and High

Priest. Thus the anointing with sacred chrism in confirmation binds us more closely to him in his regal and sacred reality.

To conclude this reflection, we might ask ourselves what effect the presence of the Holy Spirit has in our own lives. Galatians 5 is one of the great passages in the Bible where we read of the powerful presence of the Holy Spirit. Paul contrasts life in the flesh and life in the Spirit, the hallmark of the Spirit being freedom: "For freedom Christ has set us free; stand fast, therefore, and do not submit again to a yoke of slavery" (1).

But what is this Christian freedom? It is to live as Christ did, to be open and receptive to the Father in everything. In John's Gospel, Christ, in his dispute with the Jews, whom John considers to be Jesus' enemies, proclaims that freedom is not a hereditary right (see chapter 8). Rather, we are free when we are free from sin, from being turned in upon ourselves. Paul makes the same point when he defines freedom as love: "Through love be servants of one another" (Galatians 5:13). Freedom, then, means living not for our own purposes but for God and for others.

The Holy Spirit is conferred on us in baptism and confirmation so that we can realize our Christian freedom. In this sense, it is fair to see confirmation as the sacrament of Christian adulthood. Children are not autonomous but live in subjection to their parents. Adults, however, are free from this dependence. Analogously, Christian adults enter into a mature freedom, not the license to do what they want but the freedom to serve—to serve their Lord and their brothers and sisters. This is the mark of existence in the Spirit. In Paul's words, "Where the Spirit of the Lord is, there is freedom" (2 Corinthians 3:17).

Eucharist

The meal, the banquet, and the wedding feast are classical biblical images used to express God's union with humanity. In Isaiah, in the Old Testament, for example, the prophet invites Israel to the Lord's banquet: "Everyone who thirsts, come to the waters; and he who has no money, come, buy and eat! Come, buy wine and milk without money and without price" (55:1). In the Gospels, in the New Testament, Jesus tells his critics that it would be inappropriate for his disciples to fast, for the bridegroom is with them (see Mark 2:19). He also uses the parable of the wedding banquet to describe his ministry of preaching and inaugurating the kingdom of God. In Matthew 22:1, for example, we read, "The kingdom of heaven may be compared to a king who gave a marriage feast for his son."

Jesus, in fact, seems to reverence every mealtime opportunity as a sacred event. He spends much time at meals and is famous for sharing his table with tax collectors and sinners. All the Gospels, for example, record the miracle of the multiplication of the loaves; Jesus has compassion on the hunger of the people and so he feeds them. The Evangelists narrate the incident with the highly symbolic language of blessing, breaking, and distributing bread, all evocative of the community Eucharist.

Jesus also celebrates meals with his disciples, the most famous being the Last Supper. At that meal Jesus breaks bread and distributes it: "'Take, this is my body.' Giving the cup of wine to his friends, he said, 'This is my blood of the covenant which is poured out for you'" (Mark 14:22–23). With this gesture Jesus indicates his desire to offer himself as gift for his people. What he does at that meal on Holy Thursday night is a prelude to the great offering of himself that he makes the next day on Calvary.

Although John does not relate the institution of the Eucharist, he clearly knows of it. His entire sixth chapter is devoted to the discourse on the Bread of Life. The last part of this chapter is certainly eucharistic, the final verses containing the Lord's clear injunction: "Unless you eat the flesh of the Son of Man and drink his blood, you shall have no life in you" (6:53).

John's Gospel is significant for another gesture of our Lord at the Last Supper: Jesus strips himself, kneels before his disciples, and washes their feet. This is his great servant gesture. Like the eucharistic action, it is a prelude to what Jesus completes on Calvary.

Sharing the meal and washing the feet become commands of the Lord to his followers. He tells his disciples that they are to wash one another's feet. More importantly for the church's sacramental life, after instituting the Eucharist, Jesus poignantly tells his followers, "Do this in memory of me" (1 Corinthians 11:24). That this command was observed from the earliest days of the church is clear from Paul's injunctions about the Eucharist. He refers to some abuses of the church's eucharistic practice and even has his own account of the institution of the sacrament (see 1 Corinthians 11:23ff).

The church celebrates the Eucharist in memory of the Lord's command. Let us now reflect on the incredible richness of the mystery that Christian believers celebrate every time they gather at the table of the Lord. Three concepts may help us explore the abundance of this mystery: *memory*, *hope*, and *imagination*.

First, there is *memory*. We have seen the Lord's command to do this in his memory, but this command must be contextualized in the whole Jewish tradition of memory. The faith of Israel revolves around remembering God's mighty deeds, especially the great saving act of liberation from slavery in Egypt. In Deuteronomy God commands his people not to forget their history when they come into the promised land: "Take heed, lest you forget the Lord, who brought you out of the land of Egypt, out of the house of bondage" (Deuteronomy 6:12). Put in positive terms, God says, "When your son asks you in time to come, 'What is the meaning of the testimonies and the statutes and the ordinances which the Lord our God has commanded you?' Then you shall say to your son, 'We were Pharaoh's slaves in Egypt; and the Lord brought us out of Egypt with a mighty hand; and the Lord showed signs and wonders, great and grievous, against Egypt and against Pharaoh and all his household, before our eyes; and he brought us out from there that he might bring us in and give us the land which he swore to give our fathers" (Deuteronomy 6:20–23).

In the Hebrew culture, this memory is not just a recalling of things past. Rather, through memory, the past becomes the present. Each year at Passover the community proclaims, "This is the night when we were freed from slavery in Egypt. This night is different from any other night."

These concepts form the background for understanding "memory" in the Eucharist. We recall the past events of Holy Thursday and the sacrifice of Calvary. But the risen Lord, by the working of his Spirit, makes the past present;

the sacrifice is actualized here and now. It is not a new sacrifice but the once-for-all sacrifice is made present. The cross becomes present with its saving power and we are drawn into it.

Then there is the category of *hope*. We do not merely recall Christ's past deed. Rather, every Eucharist is an event of the hope of his coming again. As Paul says, "For as often as you eat this bread and drink the cup, you proclaim the Lord's death until he comes" (1 Corinthians 11:26). After the consecration in the mass, we proclaim the mystery of faith: "Christ has died, Christ is risen, *Christ will come again.*" Our eucharistic banquet is an anticipation of the heavenly banquet. In the signs of the Eucharist, we remember that our present suffering is not the last word. One day we will reign triumphant with the glorious Christ. Thomas Aquinas (1225–1274), Dominican friar and one of the most brilliant theologians of the Middle Ages, says that every Eucharist is a pledge of future glory.

Finally, we reflect for a moment on the human *imagination*. We are fed with the risen Christ; we are given the Bread of Life. But this sacramental sharing does not take place in a vacuum. Paul alerted his community at Corinth to this fact when he reminded them of those left hungry within the eucharist assembly. He admonished Christians that they cannot partake of the sacrament worthily if they close their eyes to the hungry in their midst. In our world today, there continue to be many who are hungry, who are malnourished, who suffer spiritual hunger. Thus our celebration of the Eucharist should also be a stimulus for our imagination as we ask: Where are the hungry in our midst today, the malnourished of body and spirit that we must feed? The Eucharist is a sacramental encounter with Christ but it is also a call to action. True believing leads to true acting; as we are fed with the Bread of Life, we must also give bread to the hungry on our doorstep.

Let us now briefly reflect upon two other important dimensions of Eucharist: *sacrifice* and *meal*. We alluded briefly above to the fact that the Eucharist is a *sacrifice*. Scholars tell us that although the first Christians continue to worship in the Temple, they gradually see that Christ is truly the new High Priest. The priesthood of the Old Testament was based on tribal descent and functioned in the Temple in Jerusalem. But Jesus is not descended from the priesthood of the Old Testament nor does he function in the Temple, yet he is truly our High Priest who offers the perfect, once-for-all sacrifice. As the letter to the Hebrews explains, Christ offers the perfect sacrifice because he offers himself (see Hebrews 7:27). And being both divine and human, Jesus' sacrifice is perfectly acceptable to the Father; it does not need to be repeated. As indicated above, the Eucharist is not a repetition of Christ's sacrifice but rather, a making present of that unique sacrifice here and now.

Plus, the Eucharist is a *meal*. Although much of our piety is focused on the sacrificial imagery of the Eucharist, with the presider being called a *priest*, the table being referred to as an *altar*, and the element of Christ's self-offering being indispensable to our understanding the mystery of the Eucharist, the Eucharist continues the table fellowship of Jesus. We eat and are nourished on the body of Christ. Thus the Eucharist is both sacrifice and meal—altar and table.

The Eucharist culminates in the holy communion, in the eating of the body and blood of Christ by the faithful. Here once again the sacrifice and the communion go together. The people offer the sacrifice in and through Christ and, because Christ is the perfect priest, that sacrifice is acceptable to the Father. The Father in turn gives the Son back to us, his people. The acceptance of the sacrifice results in the holy communion. In this sense the prayers of the mass often speak of a marvelous exchange between God and humanity. The total Christ, head and members, offers Christ to the Father and the Father, in turn, gives the Son back to humanity to be fed and nourished on its earthly pilgrimage.

One of the most important aspects of Catholic belief about the Eucharist is the conviction of Christ's real presence in the bread and wine. In the Middle Ages, Thomas Aquinas and other thinkers, building upon Aristotelian philosophy, coined the theory of "transubstantiation" to explain this. According to this understanding, after the words of consecration at mass, the substance is no longer that of bread and wine but of the person of Christ—although the accidents of bread and wine (their appearance, taste, smell, and physical texture) remain. Such devotions as Corpus Christi processions and benediction of the Blessed Sacrament emphasize Catholic belief in the real presence.

Undoubtedly the primary emphasis in Christ's giving us the Eucharist is food for our journey; the Lord invites us to come and eat. At the same time, Catholics find great consolation in adoring Christ in the Eucharist. Certainly this practice is rooted in the belief in his real presence. But is it meaningful to worship Christ in the Blessed Sacrament? Balthasar has suggested that the mystery of the Eucharist, both as sacrifice and meal, is so enormous, so infinitely rich in its depths, that no believer can ever fathom it. The Eucharist has, so to speak, an infinite fullness that can never fully be grasped. Adoration is the attitude of the humble believer before this unending mystery. What happens during the mass can never be fully appropriated. Thus, even beyond the mass, it is fitting to remain in awe before Christ present in the Eucharist with an attitude of profound gratitude and surrender. The only adequate response before the mystery of

Christ's unconditional self-surrender for us can be that of the "holy, holy, holy" of the heavenly angels before the Lord enthroned in majesty.

Reconciliation

In the Gospels we have many moving stories of our Lord's compassion on sinners. One is the story of Zacchaeus. Luke makes the point that Zacchaeus is not only a tax collector but the chief tax collector, a sign of how great a sinner he is considered in his culture. Yet, Zacchaeus is moved by Jesus' message; he feels the urgings of conversion. When talking to Jesus, Zacchaeus says, "Behold Lord, the half of my goods I give to the poor; and if I have defrauded anyone of anything, I restore it fourfold." Jesus, seeing these great signs of repentance, exclaims, "Today salvation has come to this house, since he also is a son of Abraham. For the Son of Man came to seek and to save the lost" (see Luke 19:1–10).

Another beautiful example of Jesus' compassion is found in the story of the woman caught in the act of adultery in John 8. Others are ready to condemn her and stone her to death. Jesus, however, rebukes the religious leaders and challenges the one without sin to cast the first stone. Then he asks her, "Woman has no one condemned you?" She replies, "No one, Lord." Jesus in turn says to her, "Neither do I condemn you. Go and do not sin again" (11).

Another moving story of how God deals with sinners is found in the Old Testament: the story of the sin of David. David, a powerful king, is smitten with lust for Bathsheba, the wife of one of his soldiers. David accosts Bathsheba in the bath and arranges to have sexual intercourse with her. Even worse, using his power, he arranges to let her husband die in battle. God sends the prophet Nathan to rebuke David and to call him to conversion. Nathan tells a parable about two men, one powerful and rich, the other powerless and poor. The rich man has many flocks and herds; the poor man has but one ewe lamb. When a traveler comes to the home of the rich man, the rich man steals and kills the poor man's lamb to feed his guest, rather than slaughtering one from his own flock. David, hearing the story, is outraged and immediately passes judgment: "That man shall die." But the prophet stuns David into recognition of his sin, declaring, "That man is you." David then confesses to Nathan, "I have sinned against the Lord" (see 2 Samuel 12).

In these biblical stories we see the essential elements of the church's sacrament of reconciliation. First, we must acknowledge our sin; we must recognize our need of conversion. Next, we open ourselves to the Lord's words of forgiveness. Finally, we go away with the intention not to sin again. We also are resolved to put right any wrong we have done to another insofar as this is possible.

In all these stories we see how reconciliation with God requires reconciliation with our neighbor. The biblical understanding of the commandments, in fact, always links the divine and the human. Jesus reiterates the teaching of the Old Testament, for example, when he enunciates the two great commandments: to love the Lord God with all our hearts and our neighbor as ourselves (see Matthew 22:36–40). These two commandments are essentially linked. We cannot love God unless we also love our neighbor. As the author of the first letter of John says, "How can you love God whom you do not see if you do not love your neighbor whom you do see?" (4:20)

In the sacrament of reconciliation then, we reconcile ourselves with both God and our neighbor. We confess our sin to God and receive God's word of forgiveness, but we also are reintegrated into the Christian community. Even our most private sins have social consequences. For sin affects who we are and, inevitably, who we are—our personhood— radiates into and affects the world. If we are filled with darkness, this affects others. Thus it is not enough to confess our sin to God; it is equally important to resolve to be converted and to make amends for the damage we have done insofar as this is possible. All this forms a part of what it means to belong to the communion of saints.

The Catholic Church celebrates the sacrament of reconciliation in three forms. One is the granting of general absolution. This form is considered exceptional. It is permitted in situations where there is danger of death or where there are not enough priests to hear individual confessions in a reasonable time. Church law requires that grave sins be confessed later in an individual confession, even though absolution has already been received.

A second form of the sacrament of reconciliation is a communal celebration of the sacrament which includes individual confession. This form underlines the communal nature of sin and conversion, and emphasizes *social sin* as well as *communal sin*. *Social sin* is the sin embedded in a culture at any given time, perhaps in ways that the culture is barely aware of. One thinks of racism, for example, sexism, homophobia, or the exploitation of poor nations by wealthy ones. Then there are the *communal sins* of a given Christian community—gossip, for example, back-biting, or the positioning of one group against another. The community can be guilty of *sins of omission* as well, such as the failure to help the poor in its midst. The communal form of the celebration of the sacrament provides an opportunity to listen to the Word of God together and to examine our consciences communally.

In this way we often get insights that we otherwise would have failed to recognize.

The third form is individual confession and absolution. Unfortunately, many Catholics have had bad experiences with confession, when priests have failed in pastoral sensitivity and penitents have felt judged rather than listened to and forgiven.

It is imperative that this form of the sacrament be celebrated as a joyful experience of God's saving mercy. The priest must give the penitent encouragement. No one should leave the sacrament feeling weighed down, discouraged, or condemned.

In our own day, the secular sphere has recognized the value of giving voice to our deepest anxieties and guilt. In psychotherapy, for example, men and women do not hesitate to reveal the darkest parts of themselves, knowing that their therapist will accept them. Something analogous can happen in the confessional, but on the level of the Spirit. Recall, again, how the Gospels reveal intense personal encounters between Jesus and sinners. Individual persons, like the woman who is caught in adultery, hear Jesus' words, "Neither do I condemn you." The same opportunity is given to us in confession today.

It is crucial that the spiritual context of the sacrament of reconciliation be observed. A rote confession of sins and a rote absolution are not the purpose of the sacrament. Rather, reconciliation presupposes a spiritual quest for conversion on the part of penitents, seeking how they can return more fully to the path of discipleship. As for the confessor, this presupposes the gifts of a spiritual guide and healer, one who can discern and help penitents see where the Lord is leading them. The sacrament of reconciliation, or penance, is about the path of discipleship. This is a long and often winding path, and disciples are likely to fall. Thus the confessor cannot bring the disciple to the goal of the journey in one single confession, nor may God's final desire for the penitent be crystal clear in a given moment. But if the confessor is a true man of the Spirit, he can listen with faith and compassion and help the penitent take the next step in the path of discipleship. It is one step at a time. The confessor's goal is to help the penitent to take that next step in discipleship.

Anointing of the sick

One of the central aspects of the ministry of Jesus is his healing activity. A beautiful example of this is found in Mark 5, the story of the woman with the flow of blood. She has exhausted her resources on doctors, yet has great faith that if she can but touch the hem of Jesus' garment she will be healed. She does, indeed, touch him, and she is, indeed, healed of her infirmity.

Jesus cures the blind man, Bartimaeus, and he opens the ears of the deaf.

When the disciples of John the Baptist are sent to Jesus to ask if he is the Messiah, he replies by citing the prophet Isaiah: "The blind receive their sight and the lame walk, lepers are cleansed and the deaf hear, and the dead are raised up, and the poor have good news preached to them" (Matthew 11:5).

When Jesus sends out his disciples to carry on his ministry, he exhorts them, "Heal the sick, raise the dead, cleanse lepers, cast out demons" (Matthew 10:8).

Before his ascension, Jesus speaks of the work of future ministers in his name: "And these signs will accompany those who believe; in my name they will cast out demons; they will speak in new tongues; they will pick up serpents, and if they drink any deadly thing, it will not hurt them; they will lay their hands on the sick, and they will recover" (Mark 16: 17–18).

Many other New Testament writings reflect on the practice of healing the sick and praying for those who are infirm. An unforgettable scene can be found in the Acts of the Apostles, where Peter heals a lame man. The man, sitting by the Temple gate, asks only for alms. But when Peter sees him, he says, "I have no silver and gold, but I give you what I have; in the name of Jesus Christ of Nazareth, walk" (3:6).

Another classic text is found in the letter of James. The author asks, "Is any among you sick? Let him call for the elders of the Church, and let them pray over him, anointing him with oil in the name of the Lord; and the prayer of faith will save the sick man, and the Lord will raise him up; and if he has committed sins, he will be forgiven" (5:14–15).

In the Bible, sickness and death are signs of the sinfulness of the human condition and our alienation from God. Because the whole biblical witness attests that God is the God of life, all that diminishes life is a sign of our separation from God. Then Christ enters into our human situation and embraces physical infirmity, weakness, and even death. His resurrection is a promise that we, too, can be victorious with him. We enter into the mystery of his suffering and death so that we can also share in his resurrection.

The sick need the healing power of Christ. The anointing of the sick by the priest is a strengthening in time of weakness. Given the unity of our bodily and spiritual reality, the sacrament can sometimes effect healing of our physical infirmity. Even when we are not healed bodily, however, the sacrament strengthens us interiorly. We know that we are not alone. Christ is with us.

In modern times, the anointing of the sick had often been reserved for the dying. Rather than a comfort, it often brought fear, for the dying person saw the arrival of the priest as a definitive death sentence. Pope Paul VI, however, revised the rite of this sacrament after the Second Vatican Council. Anointing of the sick is now given to anyone who is truly infirm, not just the dying. It is often celebrated communally, by friends and relatives gathered in a bedroom, hospital room, or church, where the sick are gathered to receive this sacrament together. It is a wonderful celebration of faith and an experience of the power of Christ in moments of great human weakness.

The ordinary minister of this sacrament is a priest, who opens the rite by laying his hand upon the sick person and praying silently. He then anoints the forehead and hands of the sick person, saying, "Through this holy anointing may the Lord in his love and mercy help you with the grace of the Holy Spirit. May the Lord who frees you from sin save you and raise you up."

This sacrament reminds us that Christ is the Divine Physician who takes compassion on us and our infirmities and who wishes to make us whole. He strengthens us in present suffering and promises that, by uniting our infirmities to his own, we will share his final victory over sin and death.

Holy orders

Recall that the seven sacraments are rooted in the life and ministry of Jesus. Traditionally, the sacrament of holy orders has been associated with the Last Supper and our Lord's words, "Do this in memory of me." But there are other moments of Christ's life that are important for holy orders. For example, Jesus comes as a prophet to preach God's Word. An important text for this aspect of his ministry is found in Luke 4: "The Spirit of the Lord is upon me because he has anointed me to preach good news to the poor" (18).

We should also remember the image of Jesus as the good shepherd. He pastures his sheep and lays down his life for his flock. Clearly, this image inspires early Christian leaders, as we see in 1 Peter, where the author exhorts presbyters: "Tend the flock of God that is your charge, not by constraint but willingly, not for shameful gain but eagerly, not as dominating over those in your charge but being examples to the flock" (5:2–3).

What is clear is that after the resurrection, the Lord provides for his church by raising up leaders to care for the community. With time and under the guidance of the Spirit, the church devises structures of ministry, partly modeled on the Jewish community and partly modeled on secular Greek culture. Unfortunately, it is difficult to know precisely all the details of the development of these emerging structures. For example, in some of the Pauline letters, like the Corinthian correspondence, it isn't clear who is in charge of the community. Certainly by the end of the New Testament period, however, a relatively firm set of structures is in place. The church is governed by an *episkopos,* or bishop, who is helped by his elders or presbyters. Deacons also are chosen especially for the ministries of charity.

This structure has remained relatively stable through the centuries, although a careful study of history will reveal remarkable variations. The Second Vatican Council devoted a great deal of thinking to church structures, especially to the role of the bishops. It is sometimes said that the First Vatican Council (1870) was the "council of the pope," defining him as universal pastor and infallible teacher. The Second Vatican Council, however, was the "council of the bishops," emphasizing the role of collegiality and the fact that the pope governs the church in union with the bishops. When the council speaks of "bishops," then, it is referring to the bishops in union with the pope as their head—often called the "college of bishops."

The Second Vatican Council also devotes much attention to the local church, that is, the diocese governed by the bishop. The bishop, in turn, is helped by his presbyterate, the priests of his diocese. Vatican II's primary image of the priest is that of the parish priest who collaborates with his bishop. Many older Catholics, of course, grew up with the idea that the priest is another Christ. They saw him principally in his sacramental functions of celebrating mass and forgiving sins. These dimensions of priesthood were stressed in modern times in the Catholic tradition because they were denied by Protestant reformers such as Martin Luther and John Calvin (1509–1564).

Vatican II, however, offers a specific document on the ministry and life of priests in the church today. The council affirms the traditional roles the ordained as *priest*, *prophet*, and *king*. As *priest*, the ordained celebrates the sacraments, especially the Eucharist. As *prophet*, he preaches the Word of God. As *king*, he governs the people of God.

What is remarkable is that the function that the council chooses to emphasize is that of preaching, or the ministry of the Word. The Council Fathers write, "The People of God finds its unity first of all through the Word of the living God, which is quite properly sought from the lips of priests" (*Decree on the Ministry and Life of Priests*, #4). By emphasizing the ministry of preaching, the council responds, in some ways, to the reformers' desire to see ministers in the church as heralds of the Word.

The council also gives considerable emphasis to the pastoral ministry of priests. Seeking to find a key that binds together all the diverse things that a priest does, the council appropriates the idea of "pastoral love" (see *Decree on the Ministry and Life of Priests*, #14). In other words, it is the love for Christ's people—the love of the Shepherd—that motivates the priest's ministry. Later, when Pope John Paul II wrote an exhortation on priestly formation, he significantly entitled it, "I will give you shepherds," drawing on an Old Testament description of the leaders of Israel.

The pre–Vatican II church, then, tended to see priests as set apart, cut off from the world, ordained especially for carrying out sacred rites and functions. The whole emphasis today is different, however. The priest is a man of the people, a leader of the community, who knows the people's problems and concerns, who can stand close to them, and who leads them to God by preaching the Word, by pastoral guidance, and by the celebration of the sacraments, especially the Eucharist. So the priesthood is not understood as being derived exclusively from the Eucharist; rather, the priest presiding at the Eucharist brings his pastoral care to completion. His ministry of preaching also flows into the celebration of the sacraments. As in the ministry of Jesus, the ordained seek to balance the ministry of deed and Word.

As the words "holy orders" indicates, the ordained in the church are persons of stability. They give structural continuity to the church throughout the ages and help the church remain faithful to the tradition handed down by the apostles.

Much of what the ordained do is to care for the Christian community. They are entrusted with the pastoral care of God's people. This can be somewhat inward-looking in that priests risk giving their time and energy exclusively to "churchly" matters and forgetting the needs of the world. But the church, as we saw in the Creed, has a missionary function: It exists for the world; it exists to evangelize. The evangelizing mission of the church, however, frequently is not done by parish clergy or even by the bishops.

This leads us to say a word about religious in the church. Not all religious are ordained, of course, but many are. In fact, the religious in the church often act as ministers on the border. They are the ones who are missionaries. They are the ones who care for fringe groups and the marginalized. One thinks, for example, of the Jesuits, with their great tradition of inculturation represented by people like Matteo Ricci (1552–1610), a scientist and Jesuit missionary to China. One thinks of groups like the Little Bothers of Jesus, who live among the people doing manual labor and preaching the gospel by their witness, often in non-Christian regions. One thinks of groups like the Missionaries of Charity, founded by Mother Teresa of Calcutta (1910–1997). These women reach out to God's most abandoned, a task that parishes are often unable to accomplish.

Church documents tend to stress the congruence of priesthood and religious life. The ideals of the religious vows of poverty, chastity, and obedience, for example, are also proposed as ideals for priestly life. Priests promise to live simply, celibately, and in obedience to their bishop. Recent documents, like the one by Pope John Paul II on consecrated life, tend to assimilate religious primarily to the contemplative model. But many religious are active and apostolic, and it is salutary for us to remember that holy orders exists to continue the pastoral ministry of Jesus. Most of us, in thinking of priests and bishops, tend to think spontaneously of parishes and dioceses. But it is important to remember that this is not the only model of priesthood. Much of the church's pastoral ministry is carried on by religious orders of men and of women—priests, sisters, and brothers. These men and women operate on the fringes and often beyond the confines of diocesan structures. Without their work, something essential to the church's mission would be lost.

Marriage

One of the most beautiful images of God in the Old Testament is that of the spouse of Israel. God freely chooses

Israel as his covenant partner and thinks of her as his beloved bride: "You shall no more be termed Forsaken, and your land shall no more be termed Desolate; but you shall be called My delight . . . and your land Married; for the Lord delights in you and your land shall be married. For as a young man marries a virgin, so shall your sons marry you, and as the bridegroom rejoices over the bride, so shall your God rejoice over you" (Isaiah 62:4–5).

The New Testament sees Christ as the bridegroom who calls us to the messianic banquet. In fact, in the period after the resurrection, the community came to see itself as the bride of Christ. Christ's relation to the church is one of complete self-giving and service. He lays down his life for the church and the church, in turn, is pledged to him in mutual fidelity and service.

The author of the letter to the Ephesians writes, "Husbands, love your wives, as Christ loved the Church and gave himself up for her, that he might sanctify her, having cleansed her by the washing of water with the word, that he might present the Church to himself in splendor, without spot or wrinkle or any such thing, that she might be holy and without blemish" (5:25–27). The author sees marriage as the mystery of mutual self-giving in Christ. The husband represents Christ in his self-offering; the wife represents the surrender of the church to her Lord. Ephesians places emphasis upon the mutuality of self-gift. Marriage is thus seen as a new reality in the light of Christ. If there is a hierarchy, it must be interpreted according to the mystery of self-giving love. As the author of the letter to the Ephesians says, "This is a great mystery, and I take it to mean Christ and the Church" (32).

Prior to the Second Vatican Council, theology tended to see marriage in somewhat institutional, even functional, terms. The ends of marriage were proposed to be mutual help and the procreation of children. Marriage was also seen as a remedy of concupiscence, that is, a way for human beings to control their sexual instincts.

The beauty of the Second Vatican Council's teaching on marriage is precisely to see marriage as a covenant—whereas an institutional view of marriage sees it as a contract. Without denying the institutional dimension of marriage, the council sees marriage primarily as the personal and mutual self-gift of the spouses. Marriage is a covenant in which a man and a woman surrender themselves totally to each other in a personal bond of union. The essence of marriage is personal commitment. The council's *Pastoral Constitution on the Church in the Modern World* speaks of the marriage covenant in this way: "Thus a man and a woman, who by the marriage covenant of conjugal love 'are no longer two, but one flesh' (Mt. 19:6), render mutual help and service to each other through an intimate union of their persons and of their actions. Through this union they experience the meaning of their oneness and attain to it with growing perfection day by day. As a mutual gift of two persons, this intimate union, as well as the good of the children, imposes total fidelity on the spouses and argues for an unbreakable oneness between them" (#48).

In this context, we can understand the three qualities of marriage that have characterized the Christian understanding of the sacrament. These qualities are rooted in the divine covenant between God and humankind in Christ.

First, marriage is monogamous. Marriage is a union between one man and one woman. Just as God gives himself totally and without reserve to his people, so husband and wife give themselves totally to each other. A polygamous marriage breaks the bond of unity and its quality of unreserved self-giving.

Second, the marriage covenant is indissoluble. In other words, it is based on an act of total fidelity. Our contemporary world is notorious for its hesitancy to make commitments; everything is provisional; all commitments can be revised. The Christian community, however, offers a great counter-cultural sign in the marriage covenant. Naturally, making marriage vows with this type of commitment is courageous. No doubt such marriage vows can seem audacious in this culture. Yet, Christian spouses make them not out of self-reliance but precisely out of their faith in God and their trust in Christ. Marriage vows are a great act of hope— hope in the future, hope for what the other can become, hope for what the couple can grow into. That is why such vows are essentially religious; they are based in God's fidelity to us, God's faithfulness to his promise. Without this basis, marriage vows would be foolhardy indeed.

Finally, we come to marriage and the procreation of children. Openness to new life, to offspring, is a requisite for a Christian marriage. Again, this can be understood in a personalist context. A love closed in upon itself is a selfish love. When genuine, however, love necessarily opens out to a third. Speaking of the fruitfulness of love, Hans Urs von Balthasar says that all genuine love bears a fruitfulness in itself that is always something of a surprise, even to the lovers themselves. That is why the arrival of a child is always greeted with the joy of the unexpected. Although families can and should be planned, procreation always remains a mystery.

Hence, the two classical ends of marriage—mutual help and the procreation of children—blend into one. A man and a woman make marriage vows out of a desire to give themselves totally to each other. This self-gift is expressed most fully in the sexual surrender of their whole persons to each other. Part of that surrender is the openness to children.

Unfortunately, Catholics often feel that the church's teaching about sex is negative. For example, when I asked a Catholic married man what he wished the church had told him about sex, he responded, "I wish some leaders in the church had told me that sex is good." This is, indeed, a legitimate desire. From Genesis onward, the fundamental biblical message is that the body is good and worthy of dignity—which includes the sexual self-expression part of marriage. It is a good thing; it is a holy thing—which does not mean that it should not be pleasurable. Sexual activity within marriage is play in the deepest sense of the word. Quoting again from the council's *Pastoral Constitution on the Church in the Modern World:* "This love is uniquely expressed and perfected through the marital act. The actions within marriage by which the couple are united intimately and chastely are noble and worthy ones" (#49).

It is to be hoped that by the witness of married couples and by more adequate and positive preaching, all Christians might come to a deeper sense of the beauty of the married vocation. By this sacrament, Christian men and women reflect to the world the love and faithfulness of Christ, as well as the goodness of the body and the positive value of sex. Sexual love is one of the most sublime experiences of God known to human beings. The church must not fail to proclaim this unequivocally.

Questions for Reflection: *Are the sacraments experiences of prayer for you? How might they become more prayerful experiences for you? How might the grace of the seven sacraments make a difference in the life of a Catholic Christian on a day-to-day basis? In addition to "receiving" sacraments, we also "celebrate" sacraments. How?*

Chapter 3

The Lord's Prayer

Our Father, who art in heaven,
hallowed be thy name.
Thy kingdom come.
Thy will be done on earth, as it is in heaven.
Give us this day our daily bread,
and forgive us our trespasses,
*   as we forgive those who*
*   trespass against us,*
and lead us not into temptation, but deliver us from evil.
Amen.

The Lord's Prayer is one of the great gifts that we receive as a Christian people, one that we too often take for granted. Yet, we should remember that it is part of our birthright as Christians. In the ancient church, the Lord's Prayer, often called the Our Father, was taught to catechumens preparing for baptism. Even today, in fact, we pray the Lord's Prayer during mass directly before communion, not during the part of the mass that is open to catechumens. Only fully initiated Christians have the right to say this prayer, for only they fully share in the Sonship of Jesus.

The petitions that constitute the heart of the Our Father are divided into two groups. The first group of petitions focuses on God; the second group focuses on our human situation.

God is implied as the subject of the first three petitions, and the form is sometimes passive, for example, "hallowed be thy name" and "Thy will be done." Scripture scholars tell us that the grammatical form of the Greek text implies that God is, in fact, the subject of these petitions. In effect, we are praying that God will sanctify his name, bring about his kingdom, and accomplish his will.

Scripture scholars suggest that we distinguish Jesus' original intent in giving us this form of prayer from later church usage. These two are not in contradiction, but there was an evolution in the church's understanding of the prayer. As we saw in our reflections on the Creed, Jesus sees his ministry as that of inaugurating the kingdom of God. He sees himself as standing at the end of the ages, awaiting a definitive in-breaking of God's rule and power over history. All of the petitions of the Our Father can be understood in this context. The first three petitions are associated with this mission of the kingdom, and the last three petitions can be interpreted in light of this mission.

But the kingdom does not come in precisely this way. Rather, Jesus is put to death and raised from the dead. In light of the resurrection, then, the church sees God's kingdom as already inaugurated in the risen Christ. The future kingdom is already present in Christ and in his church. Thus the immediate expectation of the end gradually gives way to a realization that God is offering humankind a long period of history in which his salvation will be offered to the human race through the church. Christ will reign in his church until the end, when he will place all his enemies, including death, under his feet (see 1 Corinthians 15:25). Hence, in the church's history, even beginning in New Testament times, the church begins to pray the Lord's Prayer in the light of this new understanding.

The petitions are seen not only as expressions of hope in the end time and in the definitive victory of God on the last day, however. They are also understood in their relevance for Christian daily existence, lived out in time and history under the guidance of the Holy Spirit. In our reflections on the six petitions of this prayer, we will consider both dimensions: those dealing with the final consummation of the kingdom and those dealing with God's reign in the church.

One of the forms used in the mass to introduce the Our Father is: "Taught by our Savior's command and formed by the Word of God, we dare to say." This introduction contains an important truth. Praying the Lord's Prayer is an act of boldness. Paul often speaks of *parrhesia* (boldness), a characteristic of the Christian life conferred on us by our incorporation into Christ.

What a great gift and treasure we have in being able to pray to God with the same filial attitude of trust that Jesus reveals in his prayer. Let us now look at the Lord's Prayer and analyze it line by line.

Our Father who art in heaven

God is transcendent majesty and is to be approached with fear and reverence. Jesus, however, has made it possible for us to approach God with loving trust and to call God, *Father*.

In the Old Testament the people have a tremendous reverence for the name of God, so much so that they do not pronounce it. Although in the Book of Exodus we find that God reveals his name as Yahweh, "I am who I am" (3:14), only the high priest utters that name, and then only once a year upon entering their sacred space of worship. The Hebrews are especially reluctant to apply a name like "father" to God because in a world of pagan gods, surrounded by fertility religions, the Israelites do not want to give any false impression that God has sexuality like we do.

Occasionally the Old Testament does refer to God as "father" as a way of indicating the divine election of Israel—God's love of his people and his tenderness toward her. For example, in numerous places Israel is referred to as God's firstborn son (see Exodus 4:22 and Hosea 11:1). In the Psalms we read: "As a father pities his children, so the Lord pities those who fear him" (103:13). The Old Testament also refers to God's love as maternal. One of the most moving passages is Isaiah 49: "Can a woman forget her sucking child, that she should have no compassion on the son of her womb? Even these may forget, yet I will not forget you" (15). In our own times, Pope John Paul I (1912–1978) spoke of God's love as maternal: "We are the object of the infinite love of God. We know that he always has his eyes turned toward us, even when everything seems obscure. God is our father, but even more is God our mother. God does not want to hurt us, he loves us and desires the well-being of each of us. If children become sick, they have even more right to be cared for by their mothers. And we too, if we are sick because of evil or if we find ourselves on the wrong path, we have the right to be loved by the Lord."

Despite the images of God's parental love, prayers are not normally addressed to God in this way in the Old Testament. Jesus, however, introduces this new and unique way of praying. In fact, he continually prays to God as father and addresses him with the Aramaic word *Abba*, meaning "dear father." This way of praying indicates a unique intimacy and trust. So much is this attitude characteristic of Jesus that we have his remarkable saying in Matthew 11: "All things have been delivered to me by my Father. No one knows the Son except the Father and no one knows the Father except the Son and anyone to whom the Son chooses to reveal him" (27).

By our baptism into Jesus, we are given the right to live in relationship to God in the same way Jesus does. We are privileged to call God *Abba*, Father. As Paul says, "For all who are led by the Spirit of God are sons of God. For you did not receive the spirit of slavery to fall back into fear, but you have received the spirit of sonship. When we cry 'Abba! Father!' it is the Sprit himself bearing witness with our spirit that we are children of God" (Romans 8:15–16).

So praying to the God who is "Our Father" is a sign of our new being, the new being we receive in baptism. It becomes part of our baptismal birthright. We are transferred from the kingdom of darkness to the kingdom of light. In the words of Colossians, Christ "has delivered us from the dominion of darkness and transferred us to the Kingdom of his beloved Son, in whom we have redemption, the forgiveness of sins" (1:13).

Some of the great commentators of the Renaissance, the era that rediscovered the humanism of antiquity especially through the study of ancient texts, suggest that the word *father* indicates the goodness and benevolence of God. For example, Erasmus of Rotterdam (1466–1536), a sixteenth-century Christian humanist, said that the Fatherhood of God denotes three qualities: *amor* (love), *benignitas* (goodness and gentleness), and *pietas* (spiritual affection). William Tyndale (1494–1536), an English Protestant reformer who translated the Bible into English, wrote in his *Exposition Upon Matthew 5, 6, and 7*, "You delight rather in names loving and charitable than terrible and fearful; you desire rather to be called father than lord and master; you desire that we should rather love you as your children than fear you as your servants and bondsmen. You first loved us, and of your goodness also it comes, and your reward, that we do love you again."

Human experiences of parenting can point us to the unconditional love of God, to a giving without thought of recompense. In the story of the prodigal son (see Luke 15:11–32), for example, the younger son squanders his father's resources, yet the father forgives him for no other motive than fidelity to his own fatherhood and unconditional love. When the older son refuses to enter into the feast, the father remonstrates with him saying, "All that I have is yours." If colleagueship implies collaboration and if friendship seeks reciprocity, parental love, at its best, is unconditional. So the image of God's fatherhood points to his unreserved and benevolent love. God our Father remains a gracious father, whatever our human response.

It is also no accident that this prayer addresses God as *our* Father—not *my* Father. Thus the Lord's Prayer rules out individualism and positions us in the larger human family beyond the church. Although God's fatherhood is known to Christians in a unique way through a privileged history, God remains the Father of all human beings. The entire human family is destined to be incorporated into Sonship in Christ and to know his paternal love. Hence, there is no authentic path to God that bypasses our brothers and sisters. To find God is to find and embrace the whole human family.

As the Christian community developed a full trinitarian faith, God the Father was seen to be the origin of the

Trinity. God the Father, however, was never without his Son. The very Being of the Father consists in begetting the Son in an eternal act of love. By his being relational, the Father is. But the Father has always seen us in the Son. As Ephesians says, "He chose us in him that we should be holy and blameless before him" (1:4) The Father and his love are the origin of all that we are. We are not offsprings of an uncaring universe; we are not accidents of evolution.

And, of course, the Father is the goal of our earthly pilgrimage. We know our destiny: We are all on the journey to our heavenly home. In his letter that deals with the approach of the new millennium (Tertio Millennio Adveniente), Pope John Paul II recalls the words of Jesus at the Last Supper: "This is eternal life, that they know you the only true God, and Jesus Christ whom you have sent (Jn. 17:3)." The pope comments, "The whole of the Christian life is like a great pilgrimage to the house of the Father, whose unconditional love for every human creature, and in particular for the 'prodigal son,' we discover anew each day. This pilgrimage takes place in the heart of the human person, extends to the believing community and then reaches the whole of humanity" (#49). The *Catechism of the Catholic Church* makes the same point when it reminds us that our goal in life is nothing less than heaven: "Heaven, the Father's house, is the true homeland toward which we are heading and to which, already, we belong" (#2802).

In praying to God as Father, then, we recall the origin and goal of our lives and our earthly pilgrimage. We come from God and are returning to God. But this God is no mere abstract philosophical principle or cause. Rather, God is the Mystery of unfathomable love and tenderness who chooses us for no other motive than love, who guides us with unfailing care so that we reach our destiny to dwell in his love forever.

. . . hallowed be thy name

The Bible is clear about a person's name having powerful significance: To be able to call someone by name is to have an intimacy with that person, to have a certain power over the person. Even today, some European languages make a distinction in the grammar between the familiar and the formal forms of expression. In French, for example, familiarity is expressed by *tu,* whereas formality and respect is indicated by *vous*—both translate as "you."

In revealing his name, God enters into intimacy with us. In the Old Testament, God's name is revealed to Moses as the enigmatic word *Yahweh*: "I am who I am" (Exodus 3:14). But as we have seen, Jesus reveals God to us as *Abba*, Father. In his high priestly prayer, Jesus sees his mission as precisely that of revealing to us the Father's name and so glorifying him on earth. Jesus says, "I made known to them thy name, and I will make it known that the love with which thou hast loved me may be in them and I in them" (John 17:26). We, too, glorify the name as we are incorporated into Christ and so dwell in him, thus sharing the trinitarian life.

The revelation of the name is bound up with God's plan of salvation. We have already seen that a key biblical motif is covenant. God's covenant love is faithful. In being faithful to his covenant, God is faithful to himself. Another way of expressing this is God's own fidelity to his holy name. In Ezechiel 36 we read, "Therefore say to the house of Israel. Thus says the Lord God: it is not for your sake, O house of Israel, that I am about to act, but for the sake of my holy name, which you have profaned among the nations to which you came. And I will vindicate the holiness of my great name, which has been profaned among the nations, and which you have profaned among them; and the nations will know that I am the Lord, says the Lord God, when through you I vindicate my holiness before their eyes" (22–23).

From the New Testament perspective, God manifests his holiness by destining us for Christ and redeeming us in him. Ephesians puts it magnificently: "He chose us in him before the foundation of the world that we should be holy and blameless before him" (1:4). The same passage indicates the nature of the divine plan of salvation: "To unite all things in him, things in heaven and things on earth" (10).

In this light, we can understand the sense of this first petition. We are praying that God sanctify his name definitively by bringing us that fullness of holiness to which we have been destined in Christ. This petition is obviously closely linked to the second: "Thy kingdom come." We pray that the Father will bring about the fullness of Christ's kingdom, completing the work that the Son began. The Father's holiness is vindicated and his name is sanctified when that plan, destined for the fullness of time, is brought to completion.

At the beginning of the Our Father, we recognize that this is God's work. God himself must vindicate his name and accomplish his plan of salvation. That, of course, will not happen without our cooperation. So we, too, must collaborate in this divine project and, in this way we, too, must sanctify and keep holy the divine name. In his *Sermons on the Lord's Prayer*, Saint Augustine addresses this when he writes, "Understand it aright, and it is for your own self that you ask. For this you ask, that what is in itself holy, may be hallowed in you." Reformation theologian William Tyndale speaks in the same vein. In his opinion, the petition should be understood as a prayer of this sort: "Grant now, therefore, Father, that your name on every side be glorified and that the light and glory of your name may no less appear and shine in our manners and living than it shines in the angels."

As we saw in our treatment of the Creed, Karl Rahner defined God as "holy Mystery." God is Mystery in that he transcends all our attempts to understand him. But as this first petition of the Lord's Prayer makes clear, God is *holy* Mystery—that is, God is the source of all that is good within us, the font of all our holy desires. God has placed these desires in us because he has made us for himself. Christ comes to show us that all our desires point us to our heavenly Father. In this first petition, we ask the Lord to confirm those desires in us and to fulfill them by bringing his divine plan of salvation to fulfillment. When this happens on the last day, the holiness of his name will be vindicated before the whole of creation.

Thy kingdom come

The goal of Christ's mission is a world restored to God, a world that reflects the glory of God. Speaking of the end time, Paul says, "Then comes the end, when he delivers the kingdom to God the Father after destroying every rule and every authority and power" (1 Corinthians 15:24).

In the Preface for the feast of Christ the King, we have a beautiful description of what Christ's kingdom is like. The church prays: "As king he claims dominion over all creation, that he may present to you, his almighty Father, an eternal and universal kingdom, a kingdom of truth and life, a kingdom of holiness and grace, a kingdom of justice, love and peace." Yet, when we look around at our world, we see clearly that Christ's kingdom has not yet come in its fullness. We do not see that our world is governed by the principle of truth or holiness. Nor do we see a world at peace. Injustice seems to prevail everywhere within our own country and among nations. Political life is marred by racism, sexism, abuse of women, violation of human rights, and many other types of prejudice.

In this type of world, Christians cry out to be delivered from these evils. We pray that God will bring about his kingdom. With the psalmist of old, suffering under the burden of so much evil, we cry, "O Lord, how long?" (Psalm 6:3) With the earliest Christian communities, we pray, "Maranatha"— "O Lord, come" (1 Corinthians 16:22; see also Revelation 22:20). Especially during the first weeks of Advent, when we are reminded of the fact that we do not live in a world fully redeemed, we pray for the second coming of Christ and the full realization of God's kingdom. As God's people, we cry out, longing for the fullness of redemption. It is this spirit that is echoed every time we say the Our Father and make the petition "Thy kingdom come."

In the Our Father and, indeed, throughout our Christian faith, we acknowledge that only God can bring about his kingdom. We do not of ourselves have the resources to overcome the powers of evil and to establish God's justice. At the same time, however, our trust in God and our hope in the future kingdom do not take away our own responsibility for the world. In a beautiful passage from the Second Vatican Council's *Pastoral Constitution on the Church in the Modern World,* the Council Fathers wrote, "While we are warned that it profits a man nothing if he gain the whole world and lose himself, the expectation of a new earth must not weaken but rather stimulate our concern for cultivating this one. For here grows the body of a new human family, a body which even now is able to give some kind of foreshadowing of the new age" (#39). This is also expressed clearly in the *Catechism of the Catholic Church*: "In the Lord's Prayer, 'Thy kingdom come' refers primarily to the final coming of the reign of God through Christ's return. But, far from distracting the Church from her mission in this present world, this desire commits her to it all the more strongly" (#2818).

As Christians, therefore, we have an obligation to cooperate with God's plan to work toward bringing about God's kingdom. We know that we cannot do this of ourselves, but we also know that we cannot remain idle or inert in the face of sickness, suffering, injustice, and oppression. We do what we can to create parables of the kingdom on this earth, all the while recognizing that God alone can and will achieve the final victory.

When we look back over the twentieth century, there are many outstanding Catholics who sought to create parables of the kingdom in this world. One thinks, for example, of Dorothy Day (1897–1980), the founder of the Catholic Worker movement. Besides launching the "Catholic Worker," a newspaper that promotes a Catholic presence and concern for the poor and oppressed, Day also founded a house of hospitality and a farming commune. We think, again, of Mother Teresa of Calcutta and how her entire ministry was devoted to the care of the dying destitute. The Missionaries of Charity, founded by Mother Teresa, continues to carry on her work today. There are secular examples as well, such as President John Kennedy's (1917–1963) founding of the Peace Corps. These persons and works carry on the ministry of Jesus and create tangible signs of God's kingdom in history.

The church, especially in our age, is committed to social justice and to a preferential option for the poor. The church wishes to live in a special solidarity with the marginalized and oppressed. At the same time, Christians know that political actions alone are insufficient. Evil can be eradicated only when there is a conversion of the human heart. The kingdom of God must, therefore, take root first in the human spirit. From there it begins to blossom in history as good fruit growing upon a good tree (see Matthew 7:15–20).

In praying "Thy kingdom come," we also pray for ourselves here and now. As Saint Augustine wrote in his *Sermons on the Lord's Prayer*, "We pray that it will come in us; we pray that we may be found in it." Martin Luther thought in the same way. In his *Large Catechism*, he wrote, "We pray here at the outset that all this may be realized in us and that God may be praised through his Holy Word and our Christian lives."

This petition, then, like all the others, reminds us that as Christians we live in a great tension between the "already" and the "not yet." Christ has won the victory over sin and death, but he has not yet handed the kingdom over to his Father. We live in the in-between time, in the time between Christ's resurrection and his second coming. The church, in this time, still lives in the shadow of death. As the Book of Revelation says, the church is the woman pursued by the dragon (see 12:13ff). But buoyed up by the certainty of Christ's resurrection and with eager longing for Christ's return, we move forward to his second coming, and so we cry out confidently: "Thy kingdom come."

Thy will be done on earth as it is in heaven

We have seen that in the original context of Jesus' preaching, the petitions of the Lord's Prayer refer to the definitive in-breaking of God's kingdom at the end of time. Such is also the case with our third petition.

The Greek verb that is used in the text and is translated as "be done" refers to a once-for-all unique action of God, thus making this petition a fervent prayer that God accomplish his divine plan of salvation for the human race in Christ. It reminds us of the astounding truth that our God is turned toward us; God is not God for himself alone. Rather, our God is a God of human beings. God is for us. When we pray this petition, we can think of Paul's beautiful words in Ephesians 1: "He chose us in Christ before the foundation of the world that we should be holy and blameless before him" (4). This is God's plan and we pray here that God bring it to completion so that all of us, as his dear children, may arrive at the fullness of his kingdom.

When we pray "Thy will be done" we cannot help but think of Jesus. His whole life is given over to fulfill his mission. As Balthasar said, Jesus' personhood is wholly subsumed in his mission. He is preeminently the one who is sent. His life consists in fulfilling the plan proposed by his Father—and he does this by surrendering to the inspirations of the Spirit. We see this from the beginning of his ministry when he is baptized in the Spirit, the Spirit leads him into the desert, and he inaugurates his ministry in the power of the Spirit. At the synagogue at Nazareth he proclaims the words of Isaiah 61 to be fulfilled in him: "The Spirit of the Lord is upon me, because he has anointed me to preach good news to the poor. He has sent me to proclaim release to the captives and recovering of sight to the blind, to set at liberty those who are oppressed, to proclaim the acceptable year of the Lord" (Luke 4:18–19). In our petition, then, we pray that the good work begun in the Lord Jesus will be brought to its final consummation.

As we have seen throughout, however, the church also applies the petitions of the Lord's Prayer to daily life. In this sense, we pray that we may do our part to cooperate with God's plan. We need to respond to God's initiative to inaugurate his kingdom.

"To do the will of God," however, is a phrase fraught with the possibilities of theological misinterpretation that can damage a person's spiritual life. Thus it is important to remember that our God is a God for human beings, a God of covenant love, a God on our side. Hence, God's will is always directed toward our good; God never positively wills something that would harm us. Rather, the Scripture teaches that God destines us for that heavenly banquet. Or, as the Gospel of John says, he destines us to life, not death: "I have come that they may have life and have it abundantly" (10:10).

Naturally, this does not deny the fact that we will encounter darkness in life. Christ himself, our teacher and master, confronts feelings of abandonment in Gethsemane and on Calvary. But even this darkness is integrated by God as part of Jesus' exodus to the Father. Through the cross Jesus is destined for glory—and we share the same destiny. In the dark moments of life, we pray to persevere in faith, to cling to God in spite of darkness, suffering, and death. We do this remembering the goodness of God—his promise to be with us in everything that befalls us, and his assurance that in the end he will bring us into his kingdom.

To pray "Thy will be done" is a great act of selflessness. In this petition we come to the heart of faith: to turn away from self-love to the love of God, to live not for ourselves but for others. We live out Jesus' command, "He who loses his life will save it" (Luke 9:24). This prayer brings us to the heart of the contrast between Adam and Christ: Adam, who loves himself to the point of despising God, and Christ, who loves us to the point of forgetting himself and handing over the prerogatives even of his own divinity. "He did not count equality with God a thing to be grasped, but emptied himself" (Philippians 2:6).

Our petition continues, "on earth, as it is in heaven." Heaven and earth embrace the totality of all that is. Heaven indicates where God is: his eternity within his eternal life. Earth indicates where we are: in time and history. This part of the petition reminds us that the disposition of the heart is what's important—not place. Whether in the divine life of the Trinity or on earth, Jesus is at one with the Father. Place is indifferent, for Jesus' heart is always in union with the Father. In this petition, we pray that the same may be true for us, that our heart might be anchored in God, even though we live on earth, in the pilgrimage of faith lived out in time and space. In the Creed we saw that we are made in the image of God. We also saw that Christ is the new Adam who lovingly surrenders to God in Sonship at every moment of his life. In this petition we pray that we may be conformed to the image of the Son.

With this petition we come to the end of the first part of the Our Father, the part that directly concerns God. These petitions, as we have seen, call upon God to complete his work of salvation. These petitions are a fervent prayer that God bring us the fullness of salvation. The petitions embrace three aspects of God's saving work. According to Raymond Brown (1918–1998), Sulpician priest, Scripture scholar, and biblical theologian who contributed to biblical renewal in the Catholic Church, the first petition embraces the internal aspect of God's saving work; the second petition embraces the external aspect of God's saving work; and the third petition embraces the universal aspect of God's saving work. The first prays that we glorify God's name by cherishing it in our hearts; the second prays that God's rule will be made manifest on the earth; the third prays that God's saving plan will be made visible throughout the whole of creation, both in heaven and on earth. In that day the psalmist's prayer will be realized: "Blessed be the Lord, the God of Israel, who alone does wondrous things. Blessed be his glorious name forever; may his glory fill the whole earth! Amen and Amen!" (Psalm 72:18–19)

Give us this day our daily bread

With this petition, we now move to the second set of petitions that focuses on our human situation.

There are two versions of the Our Father in the New Testament: one recorded by Matthew and one by Luke. In

Luke's Gospel, the emphasis is clearly on the request that God continue his providential care for us in daily life: "Give us each day our daily bread" (11:3). In Matthew, however, the accent is different. Matthew's text reads: "Give us this day the bread for the morrow" (6:11). Scripture scholars tell us that the Greek adjective that is translated into English with the phrase "for the morrow" is somewhat ambiguous in its meaning. However, a strong case can be made for interpreting this phrase as pointing to the banquet in God's kingdom in the end time.

As we have pointed out before, a key biblical image for God's kingdom is the banquet, especially the wedding feast of the king. In Luke 14, for example, Jesus compares the coming kingdom of God to a great banquet to which many are invited free of charge. The parable is introduced with the words, "Blessed is the man who shall eat bread in the Kingdom of God!" (15)

Many scholars also believe that the Last Supper is celebrated in anticipation of the great feast of the end time. In this last meal with his disciples, Jesus anticipates the messianic feast of the last days. This attitude is indicated when Jesus, in blessing the cup of wine, remarks, "I shall not drink again of the fruit of the vine until I drink it in the Kingdom of God" (Luke 22:18). Thus, when we pray this petition of the Lord's Prayer, we stir up our hopes to arrive at the great wedding feast of the Lamb at the end of time.

This is only one aspect of the petition, however. The other aspect is clearly underlined by Luke: "Give us each day our daily bread" (11:3). In this context, the church prays in trust that the Lord provide all that is needed on its earthly pilgrimage. This attitude of trust is typical of Luke; it is he who reports Jesus' great exhortation to trust: "Do not seek what you are to eat and what you are to drink nor be of anxious mind. For all the nations of the world seek these things; and your Father knows that you need them. Instead, seek his kingdom and these things shall be yours as well" (12:29–31).

This call to trust echoes the attitude of the people of God in the Old Testament. One thinks especially of the exodus from Egypt and the forty years of wandering in the desert. Once the people escape from slavery, for example, they begin to fear and become painfully aware of their insecurity. The Book of Exodus reports how they grumble and tell Moses of their desire to return to Egypt (see 16:1–3).

Then, as a sign of his providential care of his people, God rains down manna upon them in the desert: "I will rain bread from heaven for you . . . and the people shall go out and gather a day's portion every day" (Exodus 16:4). Because Israel does not have a larder in which to store provisions in the desert, she has to trust each night that God will provide further rations of manna the next day. The same is true for us as we pray "Give us this day our daily bread." As the

Catechism of the Catholic Church says, this petition is a call to trust "without reservation" (#2837).

As Christians, however, we can hardly pray to God for bread without thinking of the Eucharist. Notice how all four Gospels narrate the story of the multiplication of the loaves, and how all four Gospel writers indicate that Jesus does this miracle precisely out of compassion for the people. In our world today, we continue to be in need of food—food that nourishes us physically and spiritually. So Jesus gives us the Eucharist, the Bread of Life, to be food for our journey—and he does not fail to offer us this bread every day of our lives. We shall not perish, for we feed on the body of Christ. The Eucharist reminds us of the heavenly table of God's kingdom. Saint Thomas Aquinas calls the Eucharist, "a pledge of future glory."

As we pray each day for the Bread of Life, however, we cannot fail to remember all the hungry of the world, all those who suffer from any misery, especially the victims of injustice. Already in the New Testament Paul strongly rebukes the community at Corinth, since at their eucharistic feasts some go hungry while others eat in superabundance (see 1 Corinthians 11:17ff). As Pope Paul VI made clear, the light from the Eucharist must irradiate into the whole world, illuminating not only our individual lives but our ecclesial communities and, indeed, the whole of humanity. In a speech in

1976, he noted that from the Eucharist there must flow a particular style of life. The Eucharist must become a source of energy for the church's social mission, so that "the Eucharist becomes for us not only food for each of our souls, for each of our Christian communities, but also a stimulus of charity for our brothers of every race (we remember the parable of the good Samaritan) who need help, understanding, solidarity. Thus the Eucharist provides action on behalf of the social good with energy and with hope which will never be lacking so long as Christ is with us in the Eucharist."

These statements clearly emphasize the intrinsic connection between Eucharist and social love. We cannot celebrate the mystery of Christ's love without being moved with love for all of Christ's brethren, without reserve. The sacrament of the Eucharist, the sacrament of love, must become the sacrament of the poor. Just as God freely shares the heavenly bread with us in a gesture without restriction of space and time, so, too, we who share this bread must be willing to share the fruits of the earth with all God's children. As long as one of our brothers or sisters is without food or is deprived of the basic necessities of life, we cannot celebrate the Lord's Eucharist with a good conscience. Each Eucharist ends with the mission, "Go, the mass is ended," which sends us forth to labor for the just distribution of the bread of the earth among all God's children.

"Give us this day our daily bread" is a profound act of hope and trust as well as an importunate summons to create a new style of life marked by social love. God's desire to still the hunger of the human heart is paralleled by his command to fill the swollen bellies of the hungry children of the earth. Prayer for the Bread of Life and work for the bread of human hands go hand in hand.

...and forgive us our trespasses, as we forgive those who trespass against us

Jesus' command to forgive touches one of the central novelties of the New Testament; it also touches a raw nerve in the human spirit. When we have truly been injured or done an injustice, it is extraordinarily difficult to forgive.

The context of our Lord's teaching must surely be the coming kingdom of God. The Old Testament refers to the coming kingdom as the "day of the Lord." This would be a moment of judgment. John the Baptist, too, sees this as a day of God's wrath and judgment. But when we consider the ministry of Jesus, our Lord sees it as a day of his Father's mercy. He comes to proclaim the Father's forgiveness, provided his people heed his call to repent and turn back to him. We think, for example, of the man who is paralyzed, in Mark 2. Not only does Jesus heal the man's physical infirmity; he also pronounces the astonishing words, "Your sins are forgiven" (5).

In this petition of the Our Father, the small conjunctive "as" carries no minor significance, but what does the word mean? Are we making some sort of claim on God? Clearly not. Rather, we are acknowledging that we cannot ask our Father's forgiveness without the counterpart of human forgiveness. In fact, Jesus tells us that we will be in a position to receive the Father's pardon at the coming judgment if we have forgiven our brothers and sisters who have wronged us. As an example, he offers the astonishing parable of the unforgiving servant (see Matthew 18:23–34). A king has a servant who owes him ten thousand talents, an enormous sum of money—roughly equivalent to ten thousand dollars. The servant, unable to pay, begs the king's patience. Moved by the servant's plea, the king cancels the debt. In turn, this servant encounters one of his own subjects who owes him a hundred denarii—roughly equivalent to twenty cents. When this poor man is unable to pay, the servant of the king has him thrown into prison. The king, when he hears of this, is outraged. He summons his servant and delivers him to the jailers. Jesus comments, "So also my heavenly Father will do to every one of you, if you do not forgive your brother from your heart" (35).

Forgiveness is always difficult. In fact, it would be impossible, or at least very difficult, to arrive at forgiveness with our mere human resources. The king's servant gives us a good example of this. Yet, the entire New Testament teaching on forgiveness is based on the fact that each one of us has been forgiven by God. Although we are all sinners before God, although we are all guilty of taking God for granted, of forgetting God's goodness, of lacking a spirit of gratitude, God does not cease to reach out to us. The Father's mercy is given to us through his Son, Jesus Christ, who offered his life for us on the cross. The more we meditate on how much we are loved, and on how deep was the price of our forgiveness—Paul says we have been bought at a price (see 1 Corinthians 6:20)—the more we can be open to forgiving those who have offended us.

We can hardly think of Christ's command to forgive without recalling his teaching about the love of our enemies in his Sermon on the Mount. In Matthew 5 we read, "You have heard that it was said, 'You shall love your neighbor and hate your enemy.' But I say to you, Love your enemies and pray for those who persecute you" (43–44). In the Old Testament, the people of God hate the enemies of Judaism.

This is not based merely on patriotism or self-righteousness, however. Rather, the Israelites have a sense of being the chosen people. The Law is given to them by God as a way of glorifying his name on earth. Those who aim at destroying the Jewish people or its Temple in Jerusalem, therefore, are directly thwarting God's project. Hence, the Jews see hating their enemies to be a religious duty. Thus it is truly something new when Jesus tells his disciples to love their enemies.

In his work titled *The Cost of Discipleship*, Dietrich Bonhoeffer offers a beautiful meditation on the Sermon on the Mount in which he raises the rhetorical question: "Whom should we pray for if not our enemies?" He notes that these are the men and women who are precisely most in need of our prayers. He also warns us not to be romantic about this; our prayers for our enemies may not change their hearts or their attitudes toward us. In fact, our enemies may continue to do us harm. All the more reason to persevere in an attitude of prayerful supplication for those we consider our "enemies." Bonhoeffer points out that our attitude must be based on Christ's own disposition. It was the Lord who prayed for his enemies on the cross even though they continued to put him to death.

We may be tempted, however, to tell ourselves that we have no enemies, that there is no one who clearly seeks to do us harm. Perhaps, then, we need more reflection to discover that we do, indeed, have enemies. Are there persons in our life, for example, whom we find repulsive, whom we seek to avoid? Are there groups of people we dislike, who reveal to us our hidden prejudices? The key to discovering our enemies is to become more sensitive to our feelings, and any feelings of repulsion, anger, distaste, or resentment are sure signs that we are dealing with what the Bible calls our "enemies."

Feelings in themselves, of course, are neither good nor bad. We cannot control our feelings or get rid of them. In fact, the desire to get rid of certain feelings often makes them more intense. So forgiveness involves two steps. The first step is an act of our freedom in which we decide not to seek revenge against one who has hurt us and, indeed, to seek that person's good. The second step is a willingness in faith to suffer our feelings. The only way to be healed of negative feelings is to suffer them, to let them be, and to ask the Lord to purify them. Sitting with negative feelings is a painful but powerful way of moving toward purification. The *Catechism of the Catholic Church* says, "It is not in our power not to feel or to forget an offense; but the heart that offers itself to the Holy Spirit turns injury into compassion and purifies the memory in transforming the hurt into intercession" (#2843).

In fulfilling the Lord's command to forgive, therefore, we are really imitating his ministry of mercy and compassion. In the passage on forgiving our enemies, Matthew adds a saying of Jesus: "You, therefore, must be perfect as your heavenly Father is perfect" (5:48). Without repeating these words, Luke records another of Jesus' sayings: "Be merciful even as your Father is merciful" (6:36). Thus Luke interprets the command to be perfect in terms of compassion. We grow in perfection as we imitate the Lord's mercy toward us.

In his work titled *Rich in Mercy*, Pope John Paul II includes a wonderful reflection about the role of justice and mercy in God's plan of salvation. He points out that practicing justice is often not enough, because the law of justice might not bring us any further than vendetta. Our civil laws, for example, are based on the principle of retribution (the punishment must fit the crime), and we know how the penal system, incarceration, and even capital punishment often lead to the destruction of human beings. The goal of God's action, however, is always to save men and women. Precisely, then, to save a brother or sister, the law of justice must give way to the law of mercy. This is beautifully demonstrated in the parable of the prodigal son. According to justice, the father could receive the boy back not as son but as slave or hired servant. But in this way, the father still loses his son. By forgiving his child, however, he wins back a son and indeed recovers his vocation to be father. So mercy is the way in which he saves both himself and his child. The Lord commands us to act in the same way.

...and lead us not into temptation, but deliver us from evil

This petition of the Our Father has caused many difficulties for ordinary Christians throughout the ages and, as a result, has been the object of much theological reflection. The principal difficulty lies in our belief in a good and loving God. How could such a God lead us into temptation?

The resolution of these difficulties lies within the context in which Jesus lives and preaches. He lives at the end of the times, expecting the final in-breaking of God's kingdom in history. At the same time, Jesus knows that the victory of God's reign can only come about through a great contest between God and Satan, a context in which he is intimately involved.

All the Gospels attest that Jesus confronts the power of Satan in the desert. In Luke's account of the temptations, for example, after Jesus vanquishes the enemy, Satan departs for a time (see 4:13), only to return at the beginning of Christ's suffering (see 22:31). John, too, refers to Satan. In his account of the Last Supper, John says that Satan enters into the heart of Judas (see 13:27) and, when Judas departs to betray Jesus, John adds the comment, "It was night" (13:30). Surely this is symbolic of the presence of evil. The suffering of Jesus is the great contest between God and the Evil One.

Jesus tells his disciples that they must be prepared to enter into the same struggle. Although he will come again and bring about the kingdom of his Father, all this will not happen without a great contest between God and Satan—and the church will be in the midst of this conflict. The New Testament refers to this great struggle of the end time as a time of tribulation.

The Gospels present various discourses of Jesus in which he prepares his disciples for this coming contest. In Mark 13, for example, we find Jesus talking about various events that will take place "before the end." He refers to the destruction of Jerusalem and the Temple, as well as the persecution of the disciples. With this, Jesus also predicts the traumatic events of the end of the world: There will be earthquakes and wars, the sun will be darkened, the stars will fall from the sky, and the powers that are in heaven will be shaken. Commenting on these events, Jesus says two things. First, he says that unless the Lord God shortens these days, no one should be saved. Second, Christ gives the insistent warning to watch and be prepared.

This background helps us understand this petition. In the context of Jesus' preaching, this is a fervent prayer to be spared the events of this final tribulation or, at least, to be given the grace of perseverance. This petition expresses our hope to escape the destructive power of Satan, to survive the crisis preceding the definitive coming of the kingdom. It is also our fervent cry to reign at last triumphant with Christ, to share in his definitive victory over Satan.

A translation of this petition that could convey something of the original meaning Jesus gives it in the context of his preaching could be: "Save us from the time of trial but deliver us from the evil one." This translation indicates that God does not cause temptation but rather, God saves us from the wiles of Satan, especially in Satan's titanic effort to prevent the coming of God's reign.

Thus far we have reflected on this petition within the original context of our Lord's preaching. But we have seen throughout that the church also applies all the petitions of the One Father to daily life. What sense can this petition have in our daily pilgrimage of faith? One approach might be to see it as a petition for God's grace to overcome the temptations to sin that arise each day. I also prefer to see it as a prayer for the grace of perseverance. Each day we not only find ourselves struggling to be good; we also find ourselves struggling to believe. The difficulties of life are often what make faith most difficult. Our experiences of sickness, failure, weakness, the breakdown of a marriage, the tragedies of accidents, the infirmities of disease and old age—all things that have been the themes of literature throughout the ages—are the very things that can be "trials" for faith. It is easy to see the face of God in the beauties of creation and in the many blessings we receive. But in the darker moments of life, faith is put to the test. And as men and women grow older, as they face their declining years and the approach of death, it can sometimes be difficult to maintain the attitude of trust in a loving God. So amid these difficulties of everyday life, we pray that the Lord Jesus will preserve us in the graces of faith and hope.

Classical theology taught that there were two great sins against the virtue of hope: presumption and despair. In this petition of the Our Father we pray that the difficulties of life will not lead us into despair. Paul encourages us toward hope and perseverance when he writes, "If we have died with him, we shall also live with him; if we endure, we shall also reign with him; if we deny him, he will also deny us; if we are faithless, he remains faithful—for he cannot deny himself" (2 Timothy 2:11–13). Our hope is based on Christ's faithfulness to us. We do not walk alone; Christ walks with us. We only begin to despair when we feel alone. Thus we need to fix our gaze on Christ who walks with us.

I once heard a story of a Church Father who wrote, "Only he who has set his eyes on the person of the crucified Christ can persevere to the end." In other words, none of us can be certain in any one moment that we will be faithful forever; that would be presumptuous. Gabriel Marcel (1889–1973), a French Catholic convert, dramatist, and philosophical author, taught that we can commit ourselves, however, to the process of being faithful. We can pledge ourselves to fidelity one day at a time, committing ourselves to Christ amid the unknown realities that await us each day. Marcel called this *creative fidelity*. The life of Christian faith is an eminent instance of creative fidelity.

During the mass, immediately after the Our Father, the church places a prayer upon the lips of the priest that is, as it were, a continuation of the spirit of our last petition. In the name of the community he prays: "Deliver us, O Lord, from every evil and grant us peace in our day. In your mercy keep us free from sin and protect us from all anxiety, as we wait in joyful hope for the coming of our savior Jesus Christ." This is the spirit with which we end the Our Father. Freed from anxiety, we wait in hope, trusting that Christ will come again to deliver us from all harm and to bring us to the home of his Father.

Questions for Reflection: *Why is the Lord's Prayer so crucial to the faith of Christians? How does each petition of the Our Father affect the choices you make on a day-to-day basis as a Christian? Does the image of God the Father evoke for you the* *sense of trust and intimacy that Jesus experienced in his relation-ship with God? What do you think of praying to God as Mother?*

Chapter 4

The Ten Commandments

1. I am the Lord your God. You shall have
   no other gods before me.
2. You shall not take the name of the Lord your God in vain.
3. Remember the Sabbath day to keep it holy.
4. Honor your father and mother.
5. You shall not kill.
6. You shall not commit adultery.
7. You shall not steal.
8. You shall not bear false witness against your neighbor.
9. You shall not covet your neighbor's wife.
10. You shall not covet your neighbor's property.

Although the Ten Commandments were given in the Old Testament, they remain valid today. In the Old Testament, the Ten Commandments are called "the Words." This fact is important, for it reminds us that the commandments are God's Word addressed to us so that we might live fully. The Word of God, or the Law, is always understood by the people of the first covenant to be words of life, God's way of steering them from death to life. Christianity, of course, interpreted the commandments anew in the light of Christ.

When we hear the word *law* or *commandments* today, we usually think of that which restrains our liberty or autonomy. In Western democracies, where we are accustomed to developing our own destiny, we resent interference from outside bodies such as "the government" or "the state." Because such resistance makes it difficult for us to appreciate the Ten Commandments, it is important for us see the commandments in their Jewish and Christian contexts.

The commandments are given to Moses immediately after the Exodus; God has just liberated his people from slavery. The great saving deed of God is linked to God's covenant with Israel, a choice of love on God's part. The commandments express part of the response of love God expects from his people. But as part of the Law, they are part of God's guidance of his people toward life. Observing the Law of God is walking in the way of life rather than death.

Contemporary Jesuit moral theologian James Keenan has pointed out that in the Catholic tradition, the commandments have often been treated in a negative way. They have been interpreted primarily as prohibitions—how to avoid sin. When Catholic writers wanted to talk about growth in the Christian life or growth in charity, for example, they did so in their devotional writings and in treatises on the spiritual life and, traditionally, the commandments did not have a place in this literature.

Some of the reformers, however, treated the commandments not just from a negative point of view but from a positive one as well. Martin Luther, for example, followed this line in his *Large Catechism*. For him, the commandments were not just ways to avoid sin; they were also ways to grow in faith and love for God.

My treatment of the commandments is Christ-centered. I interpret each commandment as a way to love God and his Son more fully. I try to show how the commandments, fully understood, embody the essence of Christian faith.

1. I am the Lord your God. You shall have no other gods before me.

In Exodus 20 we read, "I am the Lord your God who brought you out of Egypt, out of the house of bondage. You shall have no other gods before me" (2–3). Practically speaking, God is demanding total allegiance. The Israelites should have no other gods; only the Lord who made his covenant with them and delivered them out of slavery is the true God. As I mentioned earlier, at this point of her history, Israel thought that there were, in fact, other gods, but that Yahweh, the God of Israel, was the strongest. Later, she would come to see that, indeed, the God of Israel is the only God.

Part of the first commandment, as we read it in Exodus, is a command not to have any graven images of God: "You shall not make for yourself a graven image, or any likeness of anything that is in heaven above, or that is in the earth beneath, or that is in the water under the earth; you shall not bow down to them or serve them; for I the Lord your God am a jealous God, visiting the iniquity of the fathers upon the children to the third and the fourth generation of those who hate me, but showing steadfast love to thousands of those who love me and keep my commandments" (20:4–6). This aspect of the first commandment takes on special relevance in the context of the story of Israel's' deliverance from Egypt. For shortly thereafter, while Moses encounters God upon the holy mountain of Sinai, the Israelites persuade Aaron, Moses' brother, to make them an idol that they can worship: "So all the people took off the rings of gold which were in their ears, and brought them to Aaron. And he received the gold at their hand, and fashioned it with a graving tool, and made a molten calf; and they said, 'These are your gods, O Israel, who brought you up out of the land of Egypt!' When Aaron saw this, he built an altar before it; and Aaron made proclamation and said, 'Tomorrow shall be a feast to the Lord'" (Exodus 32:3–5).

What happens in the desert surrounding Mount Sinai becomes typical of the practice of the Jewish people in their history. They are constantly tempted to abandon Yahweh and choose other gods, especially the fertility gods of Canaan. The prophets, of course, continually call Israel back to fidelity to the one true God. One of the most beautiful passages where we see this theme is in Ezekiel, where the prophet compares Israel to a young girl abandoned in childhood. A loving man finds her and takes her to himself, caring for her until she grows into the beauty of adolescence. But as she becomes aware of her beauty, and falls into the temptation of thinking that her beauty is her own possession. She forgets the man who rescued her and becomes a prostitute. Ezekiel wants to tell us that this parable represents the history of Israel with the God of the covenant. Israel's great sin is forgetfulness (see Ezekiel 16).

Then in the New Testament, when Jesus is asked about which commandment is the greatest, he harkens back to Israel's experience of God in the desert. Jesus cites Deuteronomy to tell us concisely what the first and greatest commandment is: "You shall love the Lord your God with all your heart, and with all your soul, and with all your mind, and with all your strength" (Mark 12:30). This short formula expresses, in slightly different words, what God gives to Moses as the first commandment.

Jesus not only tells us to live this commandment; he also embodies it in his own life and ministry. In John 4, he tells his disciples, "My food is to do the will of him who sent me and to accomplish his work" (34). Later, in John 8, Jesus declares, "I do what is pleasing to him" (29).

How can we express the meaning of the first commandment for our lives as Christians today? A formula that I find helpful is taken from Saint Ignatius Loyola's work titled *Spiritual Exercises*. In his "Principle and Foundation," Ignatius states simply, "Human beings are created to *praise*, *reverence* and *serve* God our Lord" (emphasis added). I find this so refreshing—to be told that the fundamental meaning of my life is praise. I am not here on earth for some functional purpose or achievement. Rather, I am here to praise God— with an attitude of praise that is rooted in acknowledging what God has done for me. I stand with the people of Israel; the salvation history that began in them reaches even to me. Just as God begins his liberating work by freeing Israel from slavery, so he fulfills it by freeing me from my sins in Jesus Christ. In Jesus, God both redeems me from sin and destines me for eternal life. Becoming aware of this, I want to praise him with all my being. I wish to sing out with the psalmist, "Bless the Lord, O my soul; and all that is within me, bless his holy name!" (Psalms 103:1)

Something similar can be said of *reverence*. This word should not convey the idea of cowering or servile obedience; God does not want the worship of slaves but of dear sons and daughters. Thus reverence is that loving awe we have before God, the same type of awe the disciples experience in the transfiguration, when they prostrate themselves before Jesus (see Matthew 17:6). Awe is a loving characteristic, an attitude based on a recognition of who God is, who we are, and the immensity of what God has done for us.

Finally, Ignatius speaks of *service*—not compulsive service but a service of gratitude to God. Our loving service of our creator never forgets the words of Jesus to his disciples, words addressed to each one of us: "No longer do I call you servants . . . but I have called you friends, for all that I have heard from my Father I have made known to you" (John 15:15).

And what about idolatry? Most of us, I am sure, are not tempted, at least literally, to worship a created idol such as the golden calf. The difficulty is, however, that we can easily turn other creatures, the things of the earth, into idols. Reformer Martin Luther once said that the human heart is a factory of idols. If we wish to know where our idols are, we should look at our desires. What do we really want? Where do we place our security? What threatens us? What would we regard as a tragic loss in our lives? What holds us back from loving God with all our hearts? Each one of us must answer these questions personally. Anything can become an idol: sex, money, career, our good name, family. The choices are infinite. It is not that these things are bad in themselves; all God has created is good. But if these things choke us, so that they asphyxiate our desire to love God above all things, then they become idols.

Correctly understood, the first commandment sums up our entire spirituality as Christians. We experience a vocation to freedom; we are not slaves to any one creature but, instead, are free to love God above all creatures and in all creatures. Moreover, aware of so many gifts received, we no longer want to live for ourselves but for God—and this not just in isolated moments but as a habitual disposition.

Ignatius of Loyola speaks of the grace of the first commandment when he asks for the grace to find God in all things. In his words, the grace we ask for is this: to love and serve the divine Majesty in everything. Such an attitude will always be more than a law or a commandment. Rather, it is truly a grace based on the recognition that God has literally done everything for us.

2. You shall not take the name of the Lord your God in vain.

The most basic presupposition for understanding the second commandment is the great respect the ancient world has for the name of another. To be able to call another by name is a sign of intimacy. It also gives the person a certain power over the other.

Israel considers it the greatest privilege to be given the name of God. In God's encounter with Moses at the burning bush, God reveals his name to be Yahweh, the Hebrew word that is often rendered into English as "I am who I am" (Exodus 3:14). The name is mysterious and indicates that, although Israel knows the name of God, she does not possess power or mastery over God. In fact, the name is rarely pronounced in Israel, a sign of the great respect that the name merits.

The commandment then has both a negative and a positive implication. Negatively, the name must not be misused. Because magic is always a temptation, especially in the ancient world, God forbids Israel from using his name in magic rites. This would be a profanation of the true relationship between God and his people, an attempt at manipulation that abuses the relation between creator and creature. Positively, the commandment enjoins Israel to have a holy reverence for the name of God. Here we should always remember that the name stands for the person. Reverencing the name of God means holding God himself in reverence. As we have seen throughout, this is also a great act of praise and thanksgiving, for it is Yahweh who chooses Israel as his people; it is God who liberates them from slavery.

Another way of looking at this commandment is that human beings are given a fundamental choice: We can bless God or curse God. Because God is our creator and redeemer, the only appropriate response to God is to bless him. The center of Jewish prayer is blessing. One blesses God for all his saving activity. This is the constant theme of the Psalms: "Bless the Lord, O my soul, and let all that is within me bless his holy name! Bless the Lord, O my soul, and forget not all is benefits" (103:1–2).

Psalm 136 is especially rich in blessings, its constant refrain being "for his great love is without end." In one verse after another, this psalm narrates all the saving deeds of God in Israel's history, each of which prompts the psalmist to praise and thanksgiving. The opening verses of the psalm set the tone:

> O give thanks to the Lord for he is good,
> for his steadfast love endures forever.
> O, give thanks to the God of gods,
> for his steadfast love endures forever.
> O give thanks to the Lord of lords,
> for his steadfast love endures forever (1–3).

The same spirit pervades many of the liturgies of the Jewish faith, paramount among them being the feast of Passover, when the Jewish people praise and thank God for their liberation from slavery in Egypt. The prayer over the bread and cup in the passover supper, for example, is essentially a great act of blessing.

The tradition of the Old Testament continues in the New. The whole of Jesus' life, in fact, is a positive embodiment of the second commandment; his whole life blesses the name of God. As we saw earlier in the Our Father, the ministry of Jesus is both a proclamation of the name of his Father and a blessing of it—and he comes that we might do the same.

As we read in John 17, Jesus says, "I made known to them thy name, and I will make it known, that the love with which thou hast loved me may be in them and I in them" (26).

In the New Testament, however, the reverence the Jewish people feel for the divine name is transferred to Jesus. The New Testament confesses that Jesus is the Lord and Savior; he is the mediator of God's presence and salvation for us. Therefore, we should hold his name in the same reverence and awe as we do his heavenly Father. Paul conveys this sense of reverence in his famous hymn in Philippians 2, which ends, "At the name of Jesus every knee should bow, in heaven and on earth and under the earth, and every tongue confess that Jesus Christ is Lord, to the glory of God the Father" (10–11). This reverence is reflected also in a passage from the Acts of the Apostles that recounts the suffering and persecution of the first apostles. In the face of this suffering, we are told that they rejoice for what they suffer for the sake of the name of the Lord Jesus (see Acts 5:41).

Christian faith is fundamentally the acknowledgment of God's covenant with us. God wants to be our God; he wants us to be his people. In making the first covenant, he reveals to us his name: Yahweh. In making the second covenant, he reveals his name as *Abba*, Father. Our lives each day seek to praise him for this revelation and to praise the name of the Lord Jesus who makes God's name known to us.

In moments of great suffering, or in moments when we feel abandoned, however, we might be tempted to curse God. This is certainly Israel's experience in the desert and in the period of exile. It is also Job's experience. But in spite of bitter experiences that reduce him to the ash heap, Job can still say, "The Lord gave and the Lord has taken away. Blessed be the name of the Lord" (1:21).

The problem of Job remains very real for us today, of course. The twentieth century has been a time of great suffering and the seeming absence of God. In his work titled *After Auschwitz* (1966), Jewish rabbi Richard Rubenstein claims that it is impossible to believe in God, given the horrors of the Holocaust. The Holocaust, he says, is the crucial theological problem of our age. The great contemporary liberation theologian of Peru, Gustavo Gutierrez, also wrote a book on Job, titled *On Job: God-Talk and the Suffering of the Innocent.* His writing is based in the sufferings of the Latin American people, people exploited by the wealthy nations of the North. Like Job in the Old Testament, these people have no one to defend them and, like Job, they cry out to God. Thus the massive disproportionate suffering of the poor masses of humanity does, indeed, raise the question of the viability of belief in God. Where is God in this world? Where can God be found?

When periods of distress and tribulation tempt us to curse God, we can see these experiences as "testings," and we can hold before us the image of Jesus who, even in the agony of the garden and on the cross, continues to bless God. Jesus knows the sufferings of humankind yet, even on the cross, he prays the Psalms, expressing both his sense of abandonment and his trust: "My God, my God why hast thou abandoned me?" (Mark 15:34 and Psalm 22:1) and "Father, into thy hands, I commit my spirit!" (Luke 23:46 and Psalm 31:5) This is the vocation of every Christian—to hold the name of God in awe and reverence, even when we feel most abandoned.

3. Remember the Sabbath day to keep it holy.

The wording of this commandment, as it is found in the Book of Exodus, reminds us immediately of a peculiarity for us Christians, for here we have a command that has been transformed in Christian history. Although the first Christians continue to celebrate the Jewish Sabbath, Christianity begins to spread to other nations. Then, after the destruction of Jerusalem, Christian worship is transferred from the Sabbath to Sunday, the first day of the week, in commemoration of the Lord's resurrection. Let us see, then, what significance the Sabbath has for Jewish faith and what significance our Sunday celebration has for us Christians.

There are two primary meanings attached to the Jewish Sabbath. First, it recalls God's rest on the seventh day of creation: "On the seventh day God finished his work which he had done, and he rested on the seventh day from all his work which he had done. So God blessed the seventh day and hallowed it, because on it God rested from all his work which he had done in creation" (Genesis 2:2–3). The commandment to keep holy the Sabbath is, therefore, an invitation to enter into God's rest. It points to the fact that the goal of creation is the eternal rest of participating in God's life. Work is not the absolute end of creation; rather, our final destiny is the enjoyment of God.

The Book of Deuteronomy also gives us a record of the Ten Commandments and, in this account, the third commandment is associated with remembering God's great act of liberating his people from slavery in Egypt. After explaining the commandment to do no work on the Sabbath, the text continues: "You shall remember that you were a servant in the land of Egypt, and the Lord your God brought you out thence with a mighty hand and an outstretched arm; therefore the Lord your God commanded you to keep the Sabbath day" (5:15). From this text we see that celebrating the Sabbath is essentially a remembering of God's mighty deeds of salvation.

Both of these meanings of the Jewish Sabbath are preserved and interpreted anew by Christian faith in light of Jesus' resurrection from the dead. All the gospel accounts agree that Jesus was raised on the first day of the week. As faith reflects on this fact, the first day of the week is seen as the eighth day, a day of fulfillment, the day on which God's purposes for the world are fulfilled. Hence, the Christian Sabbath is a celebration of the new creation as well as a day of longing for the second coming. In each Sunday celebration, we implicitly celebrate Paul's great insight: "If anyone is in Christ, he is a new creation; the old has passed away, behold, the new has come" (2 Corinthians 5:17).

But the Christian Sunday is also a day of remembering: "Christ has died, Christ is risen, Christ will come again." There is continuity here with the Jewish Passover, for Christ's death and resurrection take place precisely at the feast of Passover. The church almost immediately sees that Christ's death and resurrection is the new and definitive passover from death to life. Once again, Paul finds the right accent: "Christ, our paschal lamb, has been sacrificed. Let us, therfore, celebrate the festival" (1 Corinthians 5:7–8). So every Sunday is Easter in miniature. We recall and make present again the marvelous deed of God in freeing his Son Jesus from the dead and, with him, all of us.

What meaning, then, should our Sunday Eucharist have for us as Christians? Why has the church always considered the Sunday Eucharist so important for the Christian community? First, by inviting us to share in God's rest and by summoning us to God's feast, the church reminds us that the goal of our lives is not functional; we are not made for work. Rather, work exists for the sake of human beings. Charles Péguy (1873–1914), a French Catholic convert and socialist who sought to combine the ideals of socialism and Christian faith, lamented that in a modern capitalist culture, everything is valued in terms of economic exchange. Human talents and even the greatest human gifts, such as artistic creation and the amazing abilities of athletes, are measured in terms of marketability. The celebration of the Sabbath thus reminds us that this is not according to God's design for the creation. Keeping the Sunday worship and taking time for rest can, in these cultural presuppositions, be a great counter-cultural sign.

At this point it might be worth adding a historical note. In the history of Christianity, the prohibition against servile work on Sunday is made primarily on behalf of the serfs; the nobles and the gentry do not need to be reminded to celebrate the feast. But the church wants to protect those who are forced to work. Even today, in many cultures, it is often the poor who are practically compelled to work on Sunday. Thus the celebration of Sunday, especially when it is recognized by the laws of modern societies, can also be a step toward greater social justice by acknowledging the human need for rest.

The other important aspect of Sunday worship is "remembering": remembering that we are creatures, that we depend on God—remembering all that God has done on our behalf. God commands the Israelites not to forget all that he has done for them when they arrive in the promised land, the land flowing with milk and honey (see Deuteronomy 8:11ff). In ancient Israel the forgetting of God is often equivalent to the worship of false gods. We moderns, too, are prone to forget. We can be so comfortable that we forget that everything we have is gift. We are too often like the nine lepers who are cleansed by Jesus but who forget to return and thank him (see Luke 17:11–19).

The celebration of the Christian Sabbath is thus an invitation to rediscover our fundamental vocation to gratitude and praise. The precept of Sunday worship is a commandment of the church, but it points to something deeper, something that cannot be ordered but which flows from a personal encounter with a loving God. In his recent letter titled *The Day of the Lord*, Pope John Paul II speaks in the same vein when he writes, "More than as a precept, the observance should be seen as a need rising from the depths of Christian life" (#81). That need is the need to give thanks from a prayerful recognition that all in our lives is gift. "From his fullness we have all received, grace upon grace" (John 1:16).

4. Honor your father and mother.

With this commandment we begin the second part of the Ten Commandments. Whereas the first three commandments are directed immediately to God, the last six have to do with love of neighbor. Here we see the genius of biblical faith: the direct parallel between love of God and love of neighbor. We cannot love God whom we do not see without loving our neighbor whom we do see (see 1 John 4:20).

If many of the commandments are expressed in negative form, the fourth commandment is striking for its positive content. We are positively enjoined to honor our parents. It is interesting to note that the verb used in the Book of Exodus is *honor* and not *obey*. Honoring our parents is far broader than obeying them.

This commandment is repeated in somewhat different words in the New Testament. In Ephesians 6, for example, we read, "Children, obey your parents in the Lord, for this is right. 'Honor your father and mother' (this is the first commandment with a promise), 'that it may be well with you and that you may live long on the earth.' Fathers, do not provoke your children to anger, but bring them up in the discipline and instruction of the Lord" (1–4). Similarly, in Colossians we read, "Children, obey your parents in everything, for this pleases the Lord. Fathers, do not provoke your children lest they become discouraged" (3:20–21).

Although the Gospels preserve few sayings of Jesus about family life, Paul draws conclusions about it on the basis of his experience of Christ. For Paul, relationships in family and society should be based on the new law of self-giving and service that we learn from Jesus. Human relationships should not be based on the law of domination but on the law of love.

Children should love their parents out of gratitude. The fourth commandment makes explicit the reverence we should bear our parents because they have been our greatest benefactors. From them we receive the most precious gift we have: life itself. But from them we also receive many other benefits, such as education, care during childhood and adolescence, and very often the precious gift of faith. How can we not be grateful for these priceless gifts? Erasmus, the great

Christian humanist of the Renaissance, writes in his work titled *An Explanation of the Apostles' Creed,* "To return thanks to those through whom we have received life or recovered it pertains to piety. To return thanks to those who have first deserved well of us pertains to gratitude." In the same vein, he tells us, "After God, the highest honor is to be paid to parents, through whom he has given us this gift of life, whose care has raised us when we were otherwise doomed to perish, through whom he has educated us with a knowledge of God, the supreme parent, and elevated us to a love of him."

The fourth commandment is an example of the eucharistic attitude that is the core of the Christian way of being. Indeed immediately before speaking of family relationships, Paul lays down the fundamental principle from which all else flows: thanksgiving. "Whatever you do, in word or deed, do everything in the name of the Lord Jesus, giving thanks to God the Father through him" (Colossians 3:17).

Let us now reflect for a moment on some of the implications of this commandment for contemporary living. The command to reverence our parents is especially relevant in our contemporary Western culture where people are often viewed functionally. Unlike African and Asian cultures, where the elderly are valued for their wisdom, the elderly in our culture are often rejected as having little value—and this is not surprising. If Western cultures tend to trivialize the value of the unborn at the beginning of life, it seems to follow that they will undervalue the elderly at the end of life. Hence, ours is a society where euthanasia has an ever-growing appeal. What's more, the mobility of modern culture and a longer life expectancy often mean that the elderly are placed in assistant-living situations or nursing homes. Although this is often necessary to provide them with proper care, it is important to remember the gospel value of gratitude for our parents and the duty to honor and care for them—especially in a culture that tends to push the elderly to the margins of society.

Although Paul, in discussing the relationship between parents and children in Christ, begins with the obligation of children to parents, he nonetheless sees a reciprocal obligation of parents to children. This, too, is a salutary reminder in our culture, where dreadful examples of child neglect and abuse—sometimes to the point of death—are common stories in our daily newspapers. The principle that Paul applies to married and family life is self-sacrifice patterned after the example of Christ—a principle especially relevant for today's parents. Psychologists tell us that one of the ways parents often cause great harm to their children is by projecting onto their children their own desires, dreams, and plans—thus failing to recognize the individuality of their children. In effect, such parents attempt to create their children in their own image. Surely recognizing a son or daughter for what he or she is constitutes a most important form of self-sacrifice. Part of being a good parent is letting go of the child, letting the child reach his or her own autonomy. However painful, this is part of the pattern of Christ.

Raising children in our Western culture is notoriously difficult, especially during the time of adolescence when family harmony can be severely tested. One way of practicing the fourth commandment in our contemporary world is through dialogue and mutual listening. There is perhaps no value more needed in modern culture than listening. Children should make an effort to give their parents a chance by listening to them and thus learning from their wisdom. And parents need to listen to their children's experiences without assuming they themselves have all the answers. Take, for example, the case of adolescent sexuality. Parents are often afraid and even ashamed to talk about sex with their children, and children are afraid to ask questions. The lack of listening and dialogue about issues of sexuality can lead to extremely damaging consequences, such as unwanted pregnancies and sexually transmitted diseases. Mutual dialogue and listening may be standard pieces of advice of modern psychology, but they are also a fruitful way to embody the mutual reverence that the fourth commandment holds up as God's way for parents and children to live together in peace.

5. Thou shall not kill.

In this commandment we have an excellent example of what, at first glance, is a negative precept but whose fundamental meaning is entirely positive: This is a commandment to have a great reverence for all human life.

The foundation of this commandment is the consistent teaching of the Bible that the God of the covenant is the God of life. The God of Israel is the creator God. A beautiful passage from the Book of Wisdom teaches that God did not create death; rather, death came into the world as a result of sin: "Do not invite death by the error of your life, nor bring on destruction by the works of your hands; because God did not make death, and he does not delight in the death of the living. For he created all things that they might exist, and the generative forces of the world are wholesome, and there is no destructive poison in them; and the dominion of Hades is not on earth. For righteousness is immortal" (1:12–15).

Human life especially is to be valued. In his recent document titled *The Gospel of Life*, Pope John Paul II grounds reverence for human life in the teaching from the Book of Genesis, that human beings are made in the image of God. What is taught in Genesis is seen in a new light in the New Testament. The image of God, marred by sin, is restored in

Christ. All human beings are destined to be conformed to the image of the Son. This fact gives every human being an inestimable value. Created by God and redeemed by Christ, each human being possesses an intrinsic dignity. Pope John Paul cites the famous passage of the *Pastoral Constitution on the Church in the Modern World*, where the council states, "By His incarnation the Son of God has united Himself in some fashion with every man" (#22). The pope then comments: "This saving event reveals to humanity not only the boundless love of God, who 'so loved the world that he gave his only Son' (Jn. 3:16), but also the incomparable value of every human person" (#2.3).

The pope goes on to develop a whole theology of the gospel of life: "Whatever is opposed to life itself such as any type of murder, genocide, abortion, euthanasia or willful self-destruction; whatever violates the integrity of the human person such as mutilation, torments inflicted on body or mind, attempts to coerce the will itself; whatever insults human dignity such as subhuman living conditions, arbitrary imprisonment, deportation, slavery, prostitution, the selling of women and children; as well as disgraceful working conditions, where people are treated as mere instruments of gain rather than as free and responsible persons; all these things and others like them are infamies" (#3.3). Thus Christianity, in the words of Cardinal Joseph Bernadin (1928–1996), cardinal archbishop of Chicago and well-known spiritual leader, defends the seamless garment of life. All of life is sacred, from the moment of conception to the moment of natural death.

The Catholic Church's defense of life is well known, especially its defense of the unborn and its stance against abortion. Somewhat less well known is its teaching on capital punishment. As regards the death penalty, the pope writes, "On this matter there is a growing tendency, both in the Church and in civil society, to demand that it be applied in a very limited way or even that it be abolished completely." He continues: "It is clear that for these purposes to be achieved, the nature and extent of the punishment must be carefully evaluated and decided upon, and ought not to go to the extreme of executing the offender except in cases of absolute necessity: in other words, when it would not be possible otherwise to defend society. Today, however, as a result of steady improvements in the organization of the penal system, such cases are very rare, if not practically nonexistent" (#56.1,2).

Sister Helen Prejean, well known for her efforts to abolish capital punishment, has received international attention for her work with prisoners on death row in the United States. She has been the spiritual guide of many men and women who are condemned to die, and has even been present at a number of executions. She also has assisted the families of the victims of violent crimes. Having researched the matter, Sister Helen has shown that in the United States the victims of the death penalty are usually members of racial minorities who come from poor and violent backgrounds; the wealthy can usually afford lawyers who are able to prevent them from receiving the death penalty. She also attests that the families of victims seeking revenge for their hurt often remain in great pain, even after the offender has been put to death. She recalls the case of the father of a murdered girl who, after the execution of the offender, was still so filled with hate that he wanted to bring the man back to life so that he could kill him again. Having seen the administration of the death penalty and having first-hand knowledge of the death chamber and the procedure to put a person to death, Sister concludes that there is no humane or civilized way to put a human being to death.

If there is any clear picture of God that emerges from both the Old Testament and the New Testament it is that of a God who is a defender of the poor, the widow, and the orphan. God stands on the side of the marginalized and the defenseless. Thus it is the special mission of the church to stand on the side of those whom society often rejects as useless or of little value. In modern Western societies, these include the unborn, the elderly, the terminally ill, and the criminals on death row. The fifth commandment, especially as it is read in the light of Christ, is a fervent exhortation to us disciples to value the seamless garment of life and to defend the lives of those who have the fewest resources to defend their own lives.

6. Thou shall not commit adultery.

As with all the other commandments, the sixth commandment must be interpreted within the context of the covenant. Recall that the metaphor of marriage is often used to describe God's relationship with Israel. Thus the example of God's exclusive, faithful love for his people grounds the fidelity of human marriage and rules out adultery. In the New Testament, the covenant theology is deepened; the love between husband and wife is likened to Christ's love for the church and the church's love for him (see Ephesians 5:21–33). Just as it is unthinkable that Christ would betray his church, so is it unthinkable that the husband would betray his wife. The same is true for the church's love for her Lord and for the wife's love of her husband.

We have seen that in the theology of Vatican II, the aspect of covenant is stressed as the fundamental meaning of marriage. Marriage should be seen not so much as a legal contract but as a personal bond of commitment. Pope John Paul II has deepened this theology in numerous writings, highlighting a personal understanding of sexuality. One of the phrases he frequently uses is the "language of the body," meaning that our bodies contain their own intrinsic language. The supreme example of this is sexual union. Although man and woman are made biologically to "couple" and so produce offspring, the language of sexuality conveys something far deeper. The sexual union is the bodily expression of self-gift. In this union, a man and a woman offer themselves unreservedly to each other. The unreserved self-gift of the body expresses symbolically the self-gift of the person. Pope John Paul II says that human beings can only realize themselves in an authentic gift of self (see, for example, *The Gospel of Life*, #96.1). This is true for all persons, of course, but married persons express this self-gift in their married vows and in bodily fashion when they come together sexually.

On the basis of the theology that we have just sketched, which ultimately has its roots in God's covenant with us in Christ, the church develops her understanding of the ethics of sexuality. Without going into details, we can see the implications for Christian living. Adultery is the obvious violation of the marriage commitment because it betrays the personal bond of union between the couple. Sexual union before or outside of marriage lacks that definitive commitment which is expressed in the language of the body. In such sexual unions, persons are saying something that they don't mean. They are giving their bodies to each other, but they are not expressing an unreserved pledge. Seeking sexual gratification for oneself alone, since it is by definition turned in on itself, violates the nature of the call to an authentic gift of self. Such phenomena as prostitution and pornography are, by definition, exploitations of other persons.

Now it may seem that we are cataloging many sexual prohibitions here, but the Christian understanding of sexuality is not negative. What may seem to be prohibitions are merely the other side of the sublime call to self-gift, especially through bodily union with the spouse whom one loves unreservedly.

To return to the examples of prostitution and pornography, it is helpful to recall Paul's teaching in his first letter to the Corinthians. Shocked by some of the licentiousness of the members of his community, Paul reminds his readers that they are temples of the Holy Spirit. Christ is living in them. In their bodies they are united to Christ. Then he says, "Or do you not know that he who is joined to a harlot is one body with her? For 'the two,' He says, 'shall become one flesh.' But he who is joined to the Lord is one spirit with him" (6:16–17). Thus in prostitution, there is no real union but only exploitation. The other is not there as the focus of my self-gift but as an object for my own pleasure. The same is true for pornography, where persons are paid to perform sexual acts or where images of their body are sold so that others can be gratified by the beauty of their bodies without any reference to who they are.

One of the great insights of Christian faith is reverence for the body. This reverence is rooted first of all in the belief in the Incarnation: "That which was from the beginning, which we have heard, which we have seen with our eyes, which we have looked upon, and touched with our hands, concerning the Word of life . . . we proclaim also to you" (1 John 1:1–2). It would seem that John underscores the bodily nature of Christ's presence among us because already some were tempted to deny it. One of the earliest Christian heresies, for example, denied the real bodily presence of God among us. Thus faith in the Incarnation and, indeed, faith in the Eucharist, where the community receives Christ in the flesh, ground reverence for the body.

If we look at Paul's first letter to the Corinthians, two false understandings of the body emerge. Some members in the community evidently advocate that no Christian should marry. On the basis of baptism and the Christian's participation in the risen Christ, these Christians believe that they are already living in the end time. Hence, they should live like the angels and not engage in marriage or any sexual activity. Another group, working from the same assumptions about baptism, argue that since they are already raised, any sexual activity is permitted; the body is not important. Paul argues vehemently against both positions. Our bodies are temples of the Holy Spirit. Because of baptism, Christ dwells in us. Our union with another should express the reality of this union with Christ.

Cultures have tended to move back and forth across these two extremes—from total sexual abstinence to sexual license. Victorian society, for example, was notoriously prudish about sex and about revealing anything of the body in modes of dress. At the same time, as we know, prostitution was rife in Victorian culture, as were extreme forms of pornography. In our own time, sex is often regarded as casual fun. We have lost much of our awe before the body or the mystery of sexual union. Because our culture—for the first time in history—tends not to believe in any life beyond the present one, the body is indulged in without any hope of bodily life beyond the grave.

The Christian alternative, of course, is reverence for the body. Sex is undoubtedly good but has its own intrinsic dynamic, that of self-gift. Moreover, procreation, which is biologically connected with the fact of death and the survival of the human race, is not seen as an end in itself. Rather, every person is unique and not destined for death. He or she is called to the fullness of life beyond the grave. That is why Christianity also puts a value upon virginity. In other words, persons need not procreate biologically; they can put their hope in the spiritual fruitfulness that comes from giving one-self unreservedly to the kingdom of God. Hence, in Christianity both sexual union and celibacy are complementary values.

In this reflection we have stressed the call to bodily self-gift in sexual union. Naturally such a call is a lofty one, one that is unique and distinguishes us from other mammals. At the same time, psychologists have helped us see that we arrive at a mature response to this call through development, which is often accompanied by struggles, misunderstandings, and false starts. An adolescent's appropriation of his or her sexuality, for example, will often be marked by struggles toward self-understanding, experimentation, and mistakes. Even in adult life, there is perhaps no area of our experience where we see the fragility of our human nature more clearly than in sexuality. The church's mission, therefore, is to proclaim God's call to live a mature sexuality that expresses itself in total self-giving. Aware of human fragility, of course, the church seeks to manifest the compassion of Christ by extending mercy to sinners when they fall, helping them to rise again as they take another step along the path of discipleship.

7. You shall not steal.

Loving our neighbors implies respecting what belongs to others. Whereas the fifth commandment touches what is most essential to our neighbor, namely life itself, and the sixth commandment tells us to respect our neighbor's spouse, the seventh refers to our neighbor's property. The sense of this commandment is fairly straightforward. To take what properly belongs to another, whether it be another's possessions or earnings, is an abuse against that person. Examples of this abound in our culture, such as thefts of automobiles and break-ins into private homes. There are also large-scale violations of this commandment through embezzlement, tax fraud, investment scandals, and dishonest land deals. Our newspapers are full of tales about violations of the seventh commandment, many of them taking place on the corporate or government level.

Perhaps where we contemporary Christians need most to be sensitized is our obligation to social justice. Our obligation to our neighbor is not just an individual one; justice is not just a personal relationship between two individuals. Justice also has a social dimension.

The prophets of Israel chastise the people for their neglect of the poor and the needy. They remind the people that God abhors their worship if it is not accompanied by care for the poor. A famous example in the Old Testament is found in the words of the prophet Amos: "Woe to those who lie upon beds of ivory, and stretch themselves upon their couches, and eat lambs from the flock, and calves from the midst of the stall; who sing idle songs to the sound of the harp, and like David invent for themselves instruments of music; who drink wine in bowls, and anoint themselves with the finest oils, but are not grieved over the ruin of Joseph! Therefore they shall now be the first of those to go into exile, and the revelry of those who stretch themselves shall pass away" (6:4–7). Those who exploit the helpless, in other words, will be the first to receive God's punishment.

The letter of James in the New Testament is also an urgent reminder that Christians should show no partiality for the rich. Unless Christians take the part of the poor, their worship is in vain: "My brethren, show no partiality as you hold the faith of our Lord Jesus Christ, the Lord of glory. For if a man with gold rings and in fine clothing comes into your assembly, and a poor man in shabby clothing also comes in, and you pay attention to the one who wears fine clothing and say, 'Have a seat here, please,' while you say to the poor man, 'Stand there' or 'Sit at my feet,' have you not made distinctions among yourselves, and become judges with evil thoughts? Listen, my beloved brethren, has not God chosen those who are poor in the world to be rich in faith and heirs of the kingdom which he has promised to those who love him? But you have dishonored the poor man" (2:1–6).

Catholic social teaching over the last century has helped us see that caring for the poor is not merely a question of charity or a matter of giving alms. Rather, it is often a question of social justice. Many of the world's poor are not poor because of laziness; they are poor because they are exploited.

Catholic teaching stresses that everyone has a right to a share in the world's resources. Vatican II's *Pastoral Constitution on the Church in the Modern World* states, "God intended the earth and all that it contains for the use of every human being and people . . . the right to have a share of earthly goods sufficient for oneself and one's family belongs to everyone" (#69). If this is the case, then we cannot help but be scandalized by the lack of equality in the distribution of the world's goods. In his letter titled *On Social Concerns,* Pope John Paul II points out, for example, how there is a great inequality between the wealth of the Northern Hemisphere and the poverty of the Southern Hemisphere. Poor and developing nations are effectively exploited by rich capitalist nations. In the United States as well there are whole classes of people who do not have sufficient means even to survive. Groups such as African-Americans and Hispanics are exploited, and their poverty is connected to racism. Many immigrant workers in the United States are deprived of their human rights; they are paid unjust wages and have no resources to defend themselves. There is also the phenomenon of unemployment. Many, through no fault of their own, cannot find work and so do not even have the resources for survival. Such examples are violations of the seventh commandment. In recent writings of the Catholic Church, the pope and the bishops refer to these situations as examples of *structural sin*, that is, the exploitation of others is built into the structures of a given culture or society. The bishops call on all of us to work to change these structures.

Pope John Paul II has often called Christians to *solidarity*, a principle based on the interdependence of human beings and nations. To insure the just distribution of the world's goods, we need to recognize our interdependence. Whereas some philosophic movements in the nineteenth century and early twentieth century appealed to revolution to promote justice, the Christian vision rejects violent means to change society. Rather, faith appeals to the conversion of hearts. The Christian way is to bond with those who are poor and exploited to work together to change unjust structures. The present pope has summoned the church to a preferential option for the poor based on the principle of solidarity, which gives pride of place to the weakest members of society. It is not enough for a society to seek a just distribution of goods.

Society must look out for the weakest, those who are defenseless and unable to fight for themselves.

One cannot think of the seventh commandment without thinking of the property of others. Catholic social teaching has always defended the right of private property. In the era of communism, for example, the Catholic Church stood up prophetically against the State's invasion of privacy and defended free enterprise. At the same time, however, recent church teachings have pointed out that the right to private property is not absolute. It has to be balanced by the principle enunciated above—that there must be a just distribution of the world's resources. No individual person or nation can amass the earth's goods to the point that others are deprived of the basic necessities of life.

The seventh commandment is as valid today as it has been for thousands of years. In today's world, however, this commandment challenges us not only as individuals but also as a culture to struggle for a more equitable distribution of the earth's resources and to have a heart particularly sensitive to the needs of the weakest and most vulnerable among us.

8. You shall not bear false witness against your neighbor.

The fifth, sixth, and seventh commandments tell us to respect our neighbor's life, spouse, and property. This commandment tells us to respect our neighbor's good name. Speaking falsely of others, and thus bringing them bodily or spiritual harm, is a great violation of the Lord's command to love our neighbor as ourselves.

A striking example of the violation of this commandment can be found in the Old Testament story of Susanna (see Daniel 13). Joakim, a Jewish man, lives in Babylon and has a wife named Susanna, who bathes in her husband's garden. One day she is seen by two elders who are filled with desire for her and who proposition her to have sex with them. When she refuses, they decide to take revenge by accusing her of having committed adultery. They testify that she sent her maids away while she was bathing so she could meet a young man and have sex with him. The elders seek to have Susanna put to death for adultery, but the prophet Daniel is sent by God to defend her innocence. Daniel tricks the elders into admitting their deceit. When each elder is asked under which tree they saw Susanna, they each give different answers. In this way their treachery is unmasked and they are put to death for false witness.

In our own day, such examples of lying about others, even in grave matters, is not unknown. One thinks, for example, of the false accusation of sexual abuse that was brought against Cardinal Bernadin. In addition to such direct violations of the eighth commandment, there are many other instances in which the good name of another is damaged. Ours is an age of media frenzy in which the press seek any means to invade the privacy of others and to publicize scandals. On a lesser scale, families and communities are often torn apart by gossip that ruins reputations by innuendo—attributing motives to the actions of others without any warrant.

Especially in the climate of today's world it is salutary to read Matthew's Gospel and the Lord's directives for dealing with a wayward brother or sister: "If your brother sins against you, go and tell him his fault, between you and him alone. If he listens to you, you have gained your brother. But if he does not listen, take one or two others along with you, that every word may be confirmed by the evidence of two or three witnesses. If he refuses to listen to them, tell it to the church; and if he refuses to listen even to the church, let him be to you as a gentile and a tax collector" (18:15–17). Notice how the whole point of Jesus' teaching is to save another. Rather than destroy the reputations of others or publicize scandal about them, we should talk to them so that they might come to a true understanding of their fault. Our conversation aims at a sincere conversion.

At the beginning of his *Spiritual Exercises*, Saint Ignatius gives pointed advice to Christians which, when heeded, can do much to preserve unity of minds and hearts: "In order that the one who gives the Exercises and he who makes them may be of more assistance and profit to each other, they should begin with the presupposition that every good Christian ought to be more willing to give a good interpretation to the statement of another than to condemn it as false. If he cannot give a good interpretation to this statement, he should ask the other how he understands it, and if he is in error, he should correct him with charity. If this is not sufficient, he should seek every suitable means of correcting his understanding so that he may be saved from error." Such advice can prevent a community from being torn apart by malicious gossip.

In his insightful book on community entitled *Life Together*, Dietrich Bonhoeffer has a section on "The ministry of holding one's tongue." Bonhoeffer argues that not only must we hold our tongue from issuing falsehoods about others, but we must often refuse to say true things about others because such talk does not build up the community but tears it down. Bonhoeffer notes that Christians must often refrain from saying much that occurs to them: "This prohibition does not include the personal word of advice and guidance . . . But to speak about a brother covertly is forbidden, even under the cloak of help and good will; for it is precisely in this guise that the spirit of hatred among brothers always creeps in when it is seeking to create mischief."

For Bonhoeffer, the ministry of holding one's tongue is part of the Lord's command not to judge lest we be judged (see Matthew 7:1). It is part of accepting others as gift rather than burdens, of accepting them as they are rather than demanding that they change to conform to our expectations. This ministry is, I believe, all the more crucial in the age of mass communications, where the goal of the media is not so much the dissemination of information as the selling of newspapers. In this climate we Christians can fulfill a prophetic role if we are known for our regard for the reputation and good name of others.

9. You shall not covet your neighbor's wife.
10. You shall not covet your neighbor's property.

The ninth and tenth commandments are based on the teaching of the Book of Exodus: "You shall not covet your neighbor's house; you shall not covet your neighbor's wife, or his manservant, or his maidservant, or his ox, or his ass, or anything that is your neighbor's" (20:17).

These two commandments join with the first commandment to serve as a set of bookends at the beginning and the end of the Ten Commandments. In fact, the first commandment and the last two commandments serve as general principles for understanding the Ten Commandments as a whole. The first commands us to love God with all our heart—and from that commandment all the others follow, making concrete our love of God. The second through the eighth commandments go on to deal with our daily behaviors—our behavior in relationship with God and one another. The last two commandments bring the Ten

Commandments to a conclusion, then, by pointing to the human heart. They concern our interior dispositions, for ultimately, it is covetousness or unbridled desire that is the source of actions such as homicide, adultery, theft, and lying.

It is not just the Old Testament that condemns the sin of covetousness, however. The Gospels consistently warn against covetousness because it is an attitude of egoism, a preoccupation with self to the disregard of others. In Luke's Gospel, Jesus says, "Take heed, and beware of all covetousness; for a man's life does not consist in the abundance of his possessions" (12:15). In this context, Jesus tells the parable of the foolish man who, in his desire for comfort and security, pulls down his existing barns to build bigger and better ones. In this way he thinks to guarantee his own security—but death takes him by surprise. Jesus calls the man a fool and declares, "So is he who lays up treasure for himself, and is not rich toward God" (12:21).

In his work titled *The Institutes of Christian Religion*, Protestant reformer John Calvin comments on the sin of covetousness. He says that the point of the last commandments is "to banish from our hearts all desire contrary to love." He points out that these commandments are not only aimed at preventing actions that harm our neighbor but also positively demand that whatever we conceive, deliberate, will, or attempt should be linked to our neighbor's good or advantage.

Once again we see that although the commandments may be expressed in negative form, their meaning is thoroughly positive.

Moral theologians note that covetousness implies excessive desire. The adjective *excessive* is important for it indicates that one of the negative dimensions of avarice is its tendency to grow without restraint. Once we begin to indulge in selfish desire, we can easily become addicted; having one thing leads to desiring another. For example, sexual desires can become addictive. Our contemporary culture has made us aware of how persons' sexual appetites become more intense the more they are satisfied. The disordered heart always wants more.

The remedy against covetousness, or cupidity, is purification of the heart. Only by the purification of our desires can we grow in freedom. Saint Augustine, a master theologian and psychologist, discovered for himself how his disordered sexual desires robbed him of peace. Although he vaguely wanted to be chaste, he kept putting off the practice of chastity. In his *Confessions*, he relates how finally he was brought to conversion by God's grace. According to Saint Augustine's teachings, the will is in bondage without the medicine of God's grace; it effectively is incapable of choosing the good because it is locked in its own cupidity. God, however, comes to our rescue with his grace and frees our will to seek good and to love God above all things.

One of the beautiful effects of grace is that cupidity is purified and we begin to take delight in the good. We begin to find consolation and peace in loving God. This is the goal of living out the Ten Commandments or "the Words" of God. We arrive at what Saint Augustine called *libertas*, the freedom to be who we really are: children of God who delight in his presence and who love him in himself and in his coming to us in our brothers and sisters.

Questions for Reflection: *How might you restate each of the Ten Commandments in contemporary and positive language? Which of the commandments do you find to be the most challenging in your own life? Why? What spiritual resources might you draw on to help you faithfully live those commandments you find most challenging?*

The Beatitudes

Blessed are the poor in spirit,

for theirs is the kingdom of heaven.

Blessed are those who mourn, for they shall be comforted.

Blessed are the meek, for they shall inherit the earth.

Blessed are those who hunger and thirst for righteousness,

for they shall be satisfied.

Blessed are the merciful, for they shall obtain mercy.

Blessed are the pure in heart, for they shall see God.

Blessed are the peacemakers,

for they shall be called sons of God.

Blessed are those who are persecuted for righteousness' sake,

for theirs is the kingdom of heaven.

We have two forms of the beatitudes: one in Matthew 5 and the other in Luke 6. Matthew offers eight beatitudes; Luke offers four. Scripture scholars believe that Matthew expands Luke's account. Scholars also point out that Matthew has a tendency to spiritualize the beatitudes. For example, in Matthew we read "Blessed are the poor in spirit" (5:3), whereas in Luke we read "Blessed are you poor" (6:20). Similarly, where Matthew's text reads, "Blessed are those who hunger and thirst for righteousness" (5:6), Luke says, "Blessed are you that hunger now" (6:21). Because he is addressing those who are literally poor and hungry, Luke's account is probably closer to the original words of Jesus. Matthew, while not neglecting this dimension, also points to underlying spiritual attitudes.

The word *beatitude* is, itself, an interesting term. The spirit of the beatitudes is thoroughly Jewish; beatitudes are common in the Old Testament. One thinks, for example, of Psalm 1: "Blessed is the man who walks not in the counsel of the wicked, nor stands in the way of sinners, nor sits in the seat of scoffers; but his delight is in the law of the Lord, and on his law he meditates day and night" (1–2). Then in the New Testament, Jesus tells his disciples that they are blessed by God; they are the heirs of the divine promise, and the fullness of salvation is promised to them. When Jesus calls them "blest," he is, so to say, offering them his congratulations. They have just received the Good News!

The beatitudes are marked by contrast—the contrast between the present situation and their future reality. The future will be in marked contrast with the present. It will be a reversal of the present situation. Poverty will be replaced by fullness, hunger by satiety, mourning by gladness. Thus the beatitudes can only be understood in the context of Jesus' preaching and ministry of the kingdom. Those who receive the message of his kingdom preaching now, with joy and open hearts, will one day enter into the joy of God's reign. Their reward will be nothing less than God himself.

It would be a mistake, however, to see the beatitudes as proposing a law of moral behavior or even ethical ideals. Rather, the beatitudes express ways of living in response to the Good News of Jesus. The main actor of the beatitudes is God, who has intervened in human affairs through his Son. The most that we can do as disciples is respond.

We should also remember that in one way or another all the beatitudes refer to Jesus. He is the one who has lived the beatitudes *par excellence*. He is the poor man, the one who hungers for the righteousness of God, the pure man who seeks nothing other than his Father's will, the one persecuted and condemned to death. All the beatitudes are fulfilled in Jesus. When we seek to live the beatitudes, we are merely living out our role as Jesus' disciples. The beatitudes are patterns of discipleship. As Jesus himself said, "A servant is not greater than his master" (John 13:16). Each day we seek to hear his Good News and embody the values of his kingdom, the values enshrined in the beatitudes.

Blessed are the poor in spirit, for theirs is the kingdom of heaven

Jesus proclaims the poor as the primary addressee of the beatitudes. The Greek word for *poor* refers not to those who have little but to those who have nothing. They are the beggars of Palestine, those who daily sweat to eke out an existence but who, in spite of all human efforts, end up with nothing. In a world where being a Christian is often a sign of respectability, it is salutary to remember that Jesus' followers are the indigent, those considered the riffraff of society. We should also remember that the first Christian communities are desperately poor. In his first letter to the Corinthians, Paul says, "For consider your call, brethren; not many of you were wise according to worldly standards, not many were powerful, not many of noble birth. . . . God chose what is low and despised in the world . . . to bring to nothing things that are" (1 Corinthians 1:26–28). Reading through other letters of Paul, we see great concern to raise money for the church at Jerusalem. The original Christians simply are not the privileged of society. Even Jesus, the Son of God, is an itinerant preacher without fixed abode, family, or income. Balthasar calls Jesus the embodiment of the poor man. And who can forget Jesus' own self-description: "The Son of Man has nowhere to lay his head" (Luke 9:58).

It is just to these poor people that Jesus proclaims the inheritance of the kingdom of heaven, the word *heaven* being a circumlocution for God. Jesus says that the poor are those who know God and will have God as their future inheritance. And what is the basis for this astounding claim? Primarily it is the Old Testament conviction that God has a special love of the poor since they have no one else to defend them; God continually expresses his special care for the poor, the widow, and the orphan. God pledges his care to the people of his covenant, and this love must reach out especially to the defenseless among the people.

Poverty, of course, can crush the human spirit and is often death-dealing. Poverty can turn a person to despair and resignation. But poverty can also be an opening to faith. The poor, since they have no one else to attend to them, must look to God as their only hope. The poor, precisely because of their poverty, often turn to God as their defender. One thinks of the words of Psalm 34: "This poor man cried and the Lord heard him and saved him out of all his troubles" (6). The same psalm affirms, "The Lord is near to the brokenhearted, and saves the crushed in spirit" (18).

In today's world there are millions of people who are poor in the biblical sense. There are also many contemporary Christians who are not literally poor—without anything at all—but poor, for example, in human gifts and resources. Matthew's beatitude reminds us that if we are in this category, we must at least be poor in spirit if we are going to be disciples. Without poverty of spirit, we cannot accept the Good News of Jesus, because poverty is a symbol of the heart that is empty of self and thus open to God. Riches, on the other hand, choke the human heart (see Mark 4:18–19). If our hearts are full of ourselves, how can we be open to God? One thinks of Mary's Magnificat (see Luke 1:46–55), which is another version of the beatitudes: "He has filled the hungry with good things, the rich he has sent away empty" (1:53). Mary's empty heart enables her to receive God's Word in the Incarnation.

I think of Father Pedro Arrupe, superior general of the Jesuits from 1965–1983. He was a person who represents for me poverty of spirit. As a young man, Father Arrupe was missioned to Japan, where his openness of heart made him available to learn the great spiritual traditions of the Orient, for which he showed profound reverence. His life was indelibly marked by the atomic bombing of Hiroshima and Nagasaki at the end of World War II, when he cared for the suffering and dying. As superior general, Father Arrupe manifested great love for the church, but he tried to be open to the needs of the world as well. Living this tension brought him into difficulties with the pope. In 1981, when it looked as if he might be removed from his position as superior general, Father Arrupe suffered a stroke. Speaking out of the experience of physical and spiritual suffering, he said, "More than ever, I now find myself in the hands of God. This is what I wanted all my life, from my youth. And this is still the one thing I want. But now there is a difference: The initiative is entirely with God. It is, indeed, a profound spiritual experience to know and feel yourself so totally in the hands of God" (from "Address to the 34th General Congregation"). What a beautiful testimony of poverty of spirit.

I believe that we can sum up the entire spiritual life in the word *poverty*. Before God, each of us is poor, and we have to acknowledge ourselves as needy before God to receive God's gift. We each have many talents and gifts, but we also have limitations and weaknesses. Yet, we are not called to glory in our weaknesses for their own sake; we are not meant to have low self-esteem or be spiritual masochists. Rather, our weaknesses can be great occasions of grace that reveal to us our need of God.

Saint Thérèse of Lisieux made a great contribution to the church with her doctrine of spiritual childhood. Children know they are needy, that they cannot do everything on their own. They know they need to be led, and they know they have to rely on their parents and teachers. Therese knew that she didn't have the strength of many of God's children, but this was not paralyzing for her. She was content to be a child and thus became one of our greatest saints. Let me quote from her autobiography, *The Story of a Soul*. She raises the question about what it means to be small. She responds:

> To be small means to recognize one's own nothingness, to expect everything from God, as a small child expects everything from its Daddy. It means not worrying about anything, not winning one's own fortune. Even among the poor one gives to a child everything which he needs but as soon as he grows up, his Daddy doesn't want to nurture him but says: now you must work, you must become self-sufficient.

> Because I did not want to hear those words I didn't want to grow up. In fact I feel incapable of winning

my life, I mean, eternal life. Therefore I remained small, having no other task than that of collecting flowers, the flowers of love and sacrifice and offering them to the good God for his pleasure.

Once again, being small means not attributing to oneself the virtues one practices, believing oneself capable of something. Rather it is recognizing that the good God places this treasure in the hands of his little one so that the child can make use of what it needs. But this treasure always remains that of the good God. Finally, being small means never getting discouraged about one's defects, for children often fall but they are too small to hurt themselves.

One of Thérèse's spiritual daughters, the contemporary Carmelite Ruth Burrows, has signaled spiritual poverty as the key to the spiritual life and the essential foundation for being a man or woman of prayer, indeed for leading the contemplative life (which need not be lived in a monastery). In her work titled *Guidelines for Mystical Prayer*, she writes, "God cannot give himself to us unless our hands are empty to receive him. The deepest reason why so few of us are saints is because we will not let God love us. To be loved means a naked, defenseless surrender to all God is. It means a glad acceptance of our nothingness, a look fixed on the God who gives, taking no account of the nothing to whom the gift is made."

Awareness of our poverty is truly frightening, of course, for then we become conscious that we truly have nothing we can call our own. Recognition of this poverty also means letting go of our illusions about the spiritual life, such as our romantic fantasies about what a life of prayer would be like. The history of Christianity attests that poverty is God's way of stripping us of our illusions so that, being despoiled of our own pretensions, we can be taken possession of by Christ alone. This is the meaning of the first beatitude: Having nothing to call our own, we are promised God as our inheritance.

Blessed are those who mourn, for they shall be comforted

Leon Bloy (1846–1917), French convert to Catholicism, novelist, and journalist, said that we are called to joy. He urged us to follow those sentiments that reinforce this fundamental conviction of faith and to reject any that threaten it.

We have seen many times that the Bible speaks of the joy of God's kingdom as a "feast"; Jesus destines each of us to the joy of his wedding banquet. Weighed down by life's difficulties, however, we are tempted to forget this. Yet, our fundamental vocation is to joy. I have always found that my most intense moments of joy are those shared with another person. Joy is the spontaneous emotion we experience when we are in the presence of someone we love. God destines us to this joy because he calls each of us to an unending love relationship with him.

The Old Testament background for this call to unending joy is God's covenant of friendship with Israel. Israel's whole existence and reason for being is to bask joyfully in this covenant of friendship. Thus one of the greatest catastrophes of Jewish history is the destruction of the Temple and the Exile into Babylon. The prophets interpret these facts as punishments for Israel's unfaithfulness to the covenant, for Israel's constant sins of idolatry. The Psalms from the period of the Exile cry out, "By the waters of Babylon there we sat down and wept, when we remembered Zion. On the willows there we hung up our lyres" (Psalm 137:1–2). With the Temple gone and Israel in a foreign land, the psalmist asks rhetorically, "How shall we sing the Lord's song in a foreign land?" (Psalm 137:4)

But God does not definitively abandon his people. He sends his prophet Isaiah to console Israel, to tell her that her mourning will be turned into joy and that she will be led back to the promised land: "The Spirit of the Lord is upon me . . . to comfort all who mourn, to grant to those who mourn in Zion—to give them a garland instead of ashes, the oil of gladness instead of mourning, the mantle of praise instead of a faint spirit" (Isaiah 61:1–3).

The Christian community today is, in a sense, like the exiles of Israel. We live in the time between the death and resurrection of Jesus and his second coming. One of the images for God's definitive victory is the establishment of the heavenly city for which we are destined. When Christ returns, we will dwell in the joy of that heavenly city where, as the Book of Revelation says, there will be no need for a temple, for God himself will dwell with his people (see 21:22). Of the heavenly city, Revelation also says that God "will wipe away every tear from their eyes, and death shall be no more, neither shall there be mourning nor crying nor pain any more, for the former things have passed away" (21:4).

In Luke's version of this beatitude, Jesus promises those who weep that they shall laugh (see 6:21). Scripture scholars tell us that this is the laughter of surprise, the uncontrollable exultation of those whose misfortune has been overcome, of those who have been snatched from the menacing jaws of disaster. Jesus promises us, his disciples, that nothing can separate us from his love. The trials and tribulations we undergo in this life will give way to victory over suffering, to fullness of life over death, and to joy over sorrow. The Christian community can make its own the beautiful words of Psalm 126:

> When the Lord restored the fortunes of Zion,
>> we were like those who dream.
> Then our mouth was filled with laughter,
>> and our tongue with shouts of joy; . . .
> He that goes forth weeping,
>> bearing the seed for sowing,
> shall come home with shouts of joy,
>> bearing his sheaves with him (1, 2, 6).

We have seen that Christ is the one who perfectly lives the spirit of the beatitudes. He knows the utter darkness of the cross, but is vindicated with the glory of Easter morning. The letter to the Hebrews calls Jesus the pioneer of our faith: "For the joy that was set before him, he endured the cross, despising the shame and is seated at the right hand of the throne of God" (12:2).

We can also remember the figure of Mary, the Mother of Sorrows. One of the most moving portrayals of Mary is that of the mother beholding her dead Son, often called the "pieta." When I was a young priest in Germany, the church where I served had a beautiful baroque pieta hidden in a remote corner of the church. Parishioners frequently approached this wood carving in fervent devotion to Mary. I remember in particular a mother whose son had been killed in a motorcycle accident. How often I saw her bent over in prayer before Mary, this woman of sorrows, this woman who is a consolation for all who weep, this woman who loses her Son on Good Friday but sees him raised on Easter Day. The Sequence for the mass of Easter Sunday tells of Mary's ultimate joy: "Tell us, Mary, 'What did you see on the way?' 'I saw the tomb of the now living Christ. I saw the glory of Christ now risen.'"

Mary, then, is also a model of this beatitude. She is the one who mourns but is comforted. Her weeping is turned into laughter. The promise that Mary sees fulfilled is made also to all of us who believe. We, too, will one day come to the heavenly Jerusalem where there will be no more mourning, where every tear will be wiped away. We can be consoled by the words Paul wrote to his community in Thessalonica: "I would not have you grieve as others do who have no hope"(1 Thessalonians 4:13).

Blessed are the meek, for they shall inherit the earth

As is the case with all the beatitudes, this blessing is based on material from the Old Testament—in this instance, a verse from Psalm 37: "But the meek shall possess the land, and delight themselves in abundant prosperity" (11).

It is important to understand the word *meek* in its biblical context. Meekness is actually an equivalent of *poor* as we find the word used in the first beatitude. The meek are the powerless, those who do not count in terms of political power, those without worldly means of enforcing their rights.

We can also understand meekness in terms of humility. In the Talmud, a Hebrew interpretation of the Scriptures, we read, "Whoever humbles himself, the Holy One, blessed is He, raises him up." Understanding this beatitude in light of the life of Jesus, as we have the others, we see that here, too, Jesus embodies its meaning. He is the meek and humble one. This beatitude also reminds us of another text from Matthew: "Take my yoke upon you, and learn from me; for I am gentle and lowly in heart, and you will find rest for your souls" (11:29). One thinks as well of Paul's words about Jesus in the famous passage of Philippians 2: "Have this mind among yourselves, which you have in Christ Jesus, who, though he was in the form of God did not count equality with God a thing to be grasped, but emptied himself, taking the form of a servant, being born in the likeness of men. And being found in human form he humbled himself and became obedient unto death, even death on a cross" (5–8). Paul tells his Christians that they should have the same sentiments or attitudes that were in Christ, just as the Lord himself promised his disciples, "Whoever humbles himself will be exalted" (Matthew 23:12).

But what, exactly, is the meaning of the promise that the meek shall inherit the land? Scholars warn against interpreting this literally, as though it has to do with the land of Palestine or even the earth in a geographical sense. They also point out Matthew's tendency to spiritualize the promised land, as we read in Matthew 19 where the Lord promises his disciples, "And everyone who has left houses or brothers or sisters or father or mother or children or lands, for my name's sake, will receive a hundredfold and inherit eternal life" (29). Taken in connection with the first beatitude, this promise really concerns the kingdom of God or, in Matthew's words, the kingdom of heaven. The promise, therefore, is nothing other than the fullness of life in the presence of God.

It is difficult to preach the virtue of humility today, however, because humility in common imagination is often connected with self-abasement and a lack of self-esteem. The humble person is considered to be one who lacks gumption, one who is without real human contour. Many older Catholics, for example, will remember stories of religious who were given degrading penances so that they could learn the virtue of humility. In the film *The Nun's Story*, Sister Luke is told by her superior to deliberately fail an exam so as to win the affection of another sister who was jealous of her talents in medicine. Obviously, this idea of humility is a perversion of Christ's teaching.

I find it helpful to remember that the word *humility* comes from the Latin word *humus*, which means "ground." Humble people live close to the earth. They know the fragility of life. They know instinctively that they are neither God nor the creator of the earth. A few beautiful verses of Psalm 103 point to the truth of our human situation: "As a father pities his children, so the Lord pities those who fear him. For he knows our frame; he remembers that we are dust" (13–14).

This recognition, of course, is not meant to debase the human being. Rather, recognizing that we come from the earth and shall return to it, we acknowledge that our destiny does not lie totally in our own hands. We must rely on God and surrender to him in trust. Humble people, who acknowledge their creaturehood and thus their limitations—who let

God be God—are the very ones who are poor enough to "inherit the earth." They let God exalt them by bestowing on them the eternal life of Christ.

Blessed are those who hunger and thirst for righteousness, for they shall be satisfied

Here we see clearly how Matthew spiritualizes the more simple expression of the beatitude as it appears in Luke. In Luke's Gospel we read, "Blessed are you who hunger now, for you shall be satisfied" (6:21). No doubt Luke is thinking of those who are literally without anything to eat. Matthew, however, broadens the beatitude to emphasize our human spiritual hunger: "Blessed are those who hunger and thirst for righteousness, for they shall be satisfied" (5:6).

The background for this beatitude is Psalm 107:

Give thanks to the Lord for he is good,
for his steadfast love endures forever!
Let the redeemed of the Lord say so,

> Whom he has redeemed from trouble
> and gathered in from the lands,
>> from the east and from the west,
>> from the north and from the south.

> Some wandered in desert wastes,
>> finding no way to a city to dwell in;
> hungry and thirsty,
>> their souls fainted within them.
> Then they cried to the Lord in their trouble,
>> and he delivered them from their distress;
> he led them by a straight way,
>> till they reached a city to dwell in (1–7).

In this beatitude, our Lord praises those who search for the righteousness of God, that relationship with God that God himself desires for us. Our Lord also blesses those who long for the fullness of God's kingdom, and promises that our longing shall not go unfulfilled.

This beatitude reminds us of the importance of our spiritual desires. As Saint Augustine so beautifully said, our hearts are made for God and they shall not rest until they rest in God. Each of us has a deep hunger, a hunger that, as faith tells us, can only be satisfied by the divine; anything else will leave us disappointed and empty. Yet, our consumerist society promises that the goods of this earth can bring us happiness. In such a culture our spiritual desires can often go unde-tected; indeed, they can be snuffed out. The Scriptures constantly call us back to give space to these deepest desires, especially our hunger for God.

Praying the Psalms is a beautiful way to nourish these desires. One thinks, for example, of Psalm 63:1 ("O God, thou art my God, I seek thee: my soul thirsts for thee; my flesh faints for thee, as in a dry desert land where there is no water"), Psalm 27:4 ("One thing have I asked of the Lord, that will I seek after; that I may dwell in the house of the Lord all the days of my life, to behold the beauty of the Lord, and to inquire in his temple"), and Psalm 84:1,2,10 ("How lovely is thy dwelling place, O Lord of hosts. My soul longs, yea, faints for the courts of the Lord; my heart and my flesh sing for joy to the living God . . . For a day in thy courts is better than a thousand elsewhere. I would rather be a door-keeper in the house of my God than dwell in the tents of wickedness").

One can also think of Simeon and Anna, those beauti-ful figures who bridge the Old Testament and the New: Anna, who stands watch constantly in the Temple from her youth, and Simeon, who longs to see the coming of the Messiah. Unforgettable are Simeon's words of jubilation at having lived to see this moment of fulfillment: "Lord, now lettest thou servant depart in peace . . . for mine eyes have seen thy salvation" (Luke 2:29–30).

In this beatitude Jesus encourages us to attend to our hunger for God. Although we have seen the fullness of salvation in the coming of the Father's beloved Son, we have not yet arrived at the fullness of the kingdom. If we hope and long for the coming of the Lord, like the psalmist and like Simeon and Anna, we have the Lord's promise that we will not be disappointed. Our hunger will be satisfied without measure in the banquet of the kingdom of God.

Blessed are the merciful, for they shall obtain mercy

The constant teaching of the Bible is that God, out of the sheer goodness of his heart, has shown us abundant mercy. In his introduction to the Second Week of the *Spiritual Exercises*, Saint Ignatius of Loyola offers a meditation on the Incarnation. In that meditation, he invites retreatants to contemplate the divine Trinity looking upon the world with compassion: "We should recall how the three divine persons look at the entire surface and roundness of the world, so full of human beings. Seeing all of them going down to hell they decide in their eternal plan that the second person should become man to save the human race. In the fullness of time they send the angel Gabriel to the Virgin Mary." In his own way, Ignatius of Loyola is doing no more than echoing Paul's words in his letter to Titus: "When the goodness and loving kindness of God our Savior appeared, he saved us, not because of deeds done by us in righteousness, but in virtue of his own mercy" (3:4).

In our reflection on the Creed, when we pondered God's gracious choice of us, I offered a commentary on the biblical words for mercy in the Old Testament: *hesed* and *rahamin*. Recall that *hesed* refers to the gratuity of God's covenant choice of his people, and that *rahamin* refers to the womb of the mother who loves her child unconditionally. Here I offer a brief thought based on the German word for mercy: *erbarmen*. The derivation of this word is from medieval German, and the root of the word is *barm*, meaning "bosom." Hence, in German the word mercy is based upon the metaphor of God's taking us to his bosom; the Lord presses us to his own heart.

Jesuit moral theologian James Keenan has defined mercy as entering into the chaos of another—and God's mercy leads God to do precisely that. God enters into the mess of the human situation and becomes a human being—

one of us. He knows from within what it means to be human; nothing human is unknown to him.

Saint Anselm (1022–1109), the great medieval theologian noted for his exploration of the relationship between faith and reason, observed that it was fitting for humanity to be saved by one of its own. Anselm also knew that humanity needed God to be its redeemer. The genius of the divine plan combines both of these: God saves us—by one of us. This is the astounding miracle of the Incarnation.

The Gospels frequently state that Jesus is moved to compassion. Just as God's heart is touched by our human misery, so, too, we should open ourselves to the misery of others. We should make ourselves vulnerable to their chaos. Only in showing mercy to others can we expect God to show mercy to us. Fyodor Dostoevsky (1821–1881), Christian thinker and Russian novelist, grasped this point and expressed it magnificently in a parable in his novel, *The Brothers Karamazov*. He tells the story of a wicked lady who has done nothing good in her lifetime and so is consigned to the fires of hell at her death. Her guardian angel pleads for her but Saint Peter is unmoved. Finally, the angel persuades Peter to let the lady out of hell if she clings to an onion without saying anything evil of others. The angel holds the onion above her and she grasps it and begins to ascend. Although the onion is very fragile, it holds her. But as she ascends, others begin to cling to her and ascend with her. Still the onion holds. Then, when the woman realizes that others are trying to hold on to her onion as well, she cries out, "It's mine," whereupon the onion breaks and the woman sinks back into hell. Dostoevsky comments that, seeing the woman's ruin, the angel begins to weep.

Christ is so moved by our misery that he dies for us. He descends into the chaos of death, rises in victory over evil, and carries us with him to heaven. When we practice mercy, we are doing what God himself did before us. Doing the works of mercy is *imitatio Dei*—the imitation of God. God promises that if we let our hearts be touched by the suffering of others, we, too, will be shown mercy. Our confidence in the future is based on our response to human misery here and now.

Blessed are the pure in heart, for they shall see God

This beatitude reminds us of the fact that Jesus is a Jew and that his preaching and ministry is the definitive in-breaking of the kingdom of God into time. The background of the beatitude is Psalm 24:

Who shall ascend the hill of the Lord?
>And who shall stand in his holy place?

He who has clean hands and a pure heart,
>who does not lift up his soul to what is false
>and does not swear deceitfully.

He will receive blessing from the Lord,
>and vindication from the God of his salvation.

Such is the generation of those who seek him,
>who seek the face of the God of Jacob (3–6).

The context, therefore, is the ascent to Jerusalem and the entrance into the Temple. The psalmist asks, in effect, "Who is worthy to enter into the Lord's dwelling?" In the Old Testament, "seeking the face of God" is equivalent to being admitted into his presence in the Temple.

The general answer of the psalmist is that moral rectitude is a necessary prerequisite of authentic worship of the Lord. The psalmist would be thinking of such things as not cheating one's neighbor, not swearing falsely, not taking part in bloodshed. Simply put, keeping the commandments of God is necessary if worship is to be authentic.

Given the context of his preaching of the kingdom, Jesus is telling his disciples that integrity of life is a condition for entering into God's reign. To enter into the kingdom fully on the last day is to see the face of God, and only those who have lived lives of true integrity will be admitted.

It is also helpful to understand this beatitude in the context of Matthew's Gospel, where Jesus' teaching is frequently directed against the hypocrisy of the scribes and Pharisees. In the same Sermon on the Mount, Jesus tells his disciples, "Unless your righteousness exceeds that of the scribes and pharisees, you will never enter the kingdom of heaven" (5:20).

Another telling passage in Matthew that sheds light on our text can be found in the scathing accusations that Jesus makes against the Pharisees:

> Woe to you, scribes and pharisees, hypocrites! For you cleanse the outside of the cup and of the plate, but inside they are full of extortion and rapacity. You blind pharisee! First cleanse the inside of the cup and of the plate, that the outside also may be clean. Woe to you, scribes and pharisees! For you are like whitened tombs, which outwardly appear beautiful, but within they are full of dead men's bones and all uncleanness. So you also outwardly appear righteous to men, but within you are full of hypocrisy and iniquity (23:25–28).

These passages give us a clue to interpreting this beatitude. Jesus stresses the necessity of correct actions as well the source of our human actions by placing emphasis on the heart. Unless our interiority is pure, we will not be able to produce upright actions. A case in point is the conduct of the Pharisees that springs from a corrupt heart.

Jesus, in fact, frequently stresses the importance of the heart because the religious leaders of his time seem more concerned about correct actions in observance of the Law. For example, many of Jesus' conflicts with the religious leaders of Israel have to do with Sabbath observance. As Jesus points out, they often use the Law against the good of fellow human beings, forgetting that God gave the Law precisely to keep human beings human. Jesus says, "You have neglected the weightier matters of the law, justice and mercy and faith; these you ought to have done, without neglecting the others" (Matthew 23:23).

The Pharisees are also obsessed with ritual purity. In response to this, Jesus asks, "Do you not see that whatever goes into the mouth passes into the stomach, and so passes on? But what comes out of the mouth proceeds from the heart, and this defiles a man. For out of the heart come evil thoughts, murder, adultery, fornication, theft, false witness, slander. These are what defile a man; but to eat with unwashed hands does not defile a man" (Matthew 15:17–20).

It is often said that Matthew's Gospel presents Jesus as the Teacher, the New Moses, the one who gives the Law of the new covenant. Indeed, Jesus says that he did not come to abolish the

Law but to bring it to fulfillment (see Matthew 5:17). Matthew stresses that true disciples must put into practice the Lord's teaching; their lives must correspond to their beliefs. Again in Matthew we hear Jesus' words, "Not everyone who says to me 'Lord, Lord' shall enter into the kingdom of heaven, but he who does the will of my Father who is in heaven" (7:21).

Because Jesus fulfills the Old Testament sense of the Law by underscoring the importance of the heart, his followers will be marked by integrity of heart. The gospel will transform his followers interiorly, and so their actions will reflect the desires of their heart. All danger of hypocrisy will thus be excluded. Living in this beautiful correspondence between the interior and the exterior, Jesus' disciples receive a beautiful promise: nothing less than the vision of God face to face!

Blessed are the peacemakers, for they shall be called sons of God

The word *peace* in the Bible is a term with a far richer significance than our English word suggests. The peace that Jesus speaks of is the Shalom of God, a peace that comes about when we have a right relationship with God. Because of this correct relationship, we are not only at peace with ourselves, but this peace overflows into our relationships with our neighbor and, indeed, with the whole cosmos.

Christ brings about peace between God and humankind. As Paul says in his letter to the Ephesians, Christ has broken down the walls of division (see 2:14), and one of the greatest divisions that Paul is aware of is that between Jews and Gentiles. Yet, because of Christ's death, a death for all, even that division is overcome: "For he is our peace, who has made us both one, and has broken down the dividing wall of hostility, by abolishing in his flesh the law of commandments and ordinances, that he might create in himself one new man in place of two, so making peace, and might reconcile us both to God in one body through the cross thereby bringing the hostility to an end" (2:14–16).

At the Last Supper, Christ promises his peace: "Peace I leave you, my peace I give you. Not as the world gives, do I give to you" (John 14:27). We have Christ's peace in us because we have received the gift of the Holy Spirit. As we saw in our reflections on the Creed, because of the Spirit we are in communion with God. We have that relationship with God that the Father wants and that Christ made possible.

In one of Bonhoeffer's meditations upon the beatitudes, he notes that we have peace because of Christ's gift and that we must be makers of peace. We see this same idea in Jesus' beatitude as it is echoed in Psalm 34: "Depart from evil and do good; seek peace and pursue it" (14). A Jewish tradition speaks in the same way. According to the rabbis, all commandments are to be fulfilled when the right opportunity arrives—but not peace! Peace we must seek out and pursue.

Yet, the hostility that exists within families, the continual wars between nations, and the experience of genocide are obvious signs indicating that God's kingdom has not, in fact, come in its fullness; we do not yet live in and with peace. It is the way of the evil spirit to stir up seeds of dissension and mistrust that lead to violence, psychologically and physically. Carlo Maria Martini, contemporary biblical theologian and writer on Christian spirituality, says that the human being is made with an intrinsic desire to communicate, but the evil spirit does everything to block the realization of this desire. In his work titled *Ritrovare se stessi* (*On Rediscovering Yourself*), he speaks of the temptation of Adam and Eve and notes that the evil spirit as liar insinuates "a suspicion, a temptation which continues every day in history and pervades every human environment. Friendships are ruptured, families separated, contacts broken, and the most sacred pacts among nations violated. Thus divisions occur, social communication is perverted, information is falsified or exaggerated. Mistaken, imperfect and deviating communication is based upon ruptures among persons and groups. And the fault does not lie simply with the mass media."

In modern Western societies like our own, the breakdown of the family is manifested in many ways: bitter divorces, spouse and child abuse, and family feuds based upon avarice. Dissension between the sexes manifests itself in sexual harassment, and family disagreements often end with one member shooting another. Our schools have become unsafe as children now take weapons to class, and our newspapers are filled with tales of terrorism and warfare. Sadly, it is often the innocent, especially children, who are the victims of this violence. Recent genocides, such as that witnessed in Rwanda in 1994 and Kosovo in 1999, arouse horror when we see the devastating consequences that the hatred of the human heart can wreak. Jesus tells us that if we wish to be his disciples, we must resist this violence with every fiber of our being—and the way of Jesus is not that of resisting with bloodshed but the art of peacemaking.

We have seen throughout that the beatitudes are promises reserved for the last day. The peaceable kingdom that Jesus comes to bring about will be fully realized only when Christ comes again and hands over his kingdom to the Father. The poetic images of Isaiah that we often associate with Advent and the arrival of the Christmas season give us hints of what that kingdom of universal peace will be like. Speaking of the messianic reign, Isaiah says:

> He shall judge between the nations,
>> and shall decide for many peoples;
> and they shall beat their swords into plowshares,
>> and their spears into pruning hooks;
> nation shall not lift up sword against nation,
>> neither shall they learn war any more (2:4).

The peace of the messianic kingdom will be so extensive as to embrace even the animals; even the violence of the animal kingdom and the threat of animals to humankind will be overcome. The same Isaiah describes the peaceable kingdom in these terms:

> The wolf shall dwell with the lamb,
>> and the leopard shall lie down with the kid,
> and the calf and the lion and the fatling together,
>> and a little child shall lead them.
> The cow and the bear shall feed;
>> their young shall lie down together;
>> and the lion shall eat straw like the ox.
> The sucking child shall play over the hole of the
>> asp

> and the weaned child shall put his hand on the
> > adder's den.
> They shall not hurt or destroy
> > in all my holy mountain;
> for the earth shall be full of the knowledge of the
> > Lord
> > as the waters cover the sea (11:6–9).

Obviously, these images reveal that this type of peace will never be realized in the world as we know it. Rather, this is the peace of the final day. Nevertheless, the images are meant to stir up our hope and our longing, and to serve as stimuli for actions here and now. We who hope for the peaceable kingdom must become the peacemakers. We must work on earth to bring about the peace of God's kingdom.

This beatitude promises that the peacemakers shall be called "sons" of God, echoing a passage in the Book of Genesis, where the "sons" of God become enamored of the daughters of men. Although this strange incident in Genesis 6 is probably influenced by pagan mythology, the sons of God referred to are angels or semi-divine beings who minister in the divine court. Hence, we have another inference that the promise made by Jesus is reserved for the kingdom of heaven, when the disciples—men and women—will be admitted to the divine presence. As Christians we see Jesus as the Son *par excellence* who intimately knows his *Abba*, Father. Sharing that Sonship is the privilege of all his disciples. When we follow Jesus and put into practice his teaching—when we become peacemakers following him who is the King of Peace—we have the certain assurance that we, too, will reign with him as sons and daughters in the kingdom of the Father. Being a child of God is never something we should take for granted. It is a gift that brings disciples the promise of an eternal inheritance.

Blessed are those who are persecuted for righteousness' sake, for theirs is the kingdom of heaven

In the Old Testament God's righteousness, or justice, is a saving righteousness. God places himself in a covenant of love with Israel, the covenant being the right relationship that God wishes to have with us. God is just by being faithful to himself, and his actions on our behalf are meant to restore the covenant when it is destroyed from the human side by sin.

Jesus is the sun of righteousness. He embodies God's justice. He shows us the right way to walk before God. We live in God's justice when we live Jesus' filial relationship to the Father, and Jesus gives his life that we might know this new existence of living in God's saving justice.

Yet, all the Gospels recount that, for some mysterious reason, God's saving offer meets with human resistance and even rejection; Jesus' ministry constantly meets growing opposition. There is a terrible clash between light and darkness, and the darkness of evil ultimately brings Jesus to the cross. He who embodies divine righteousness is put to death by the powers of evil. Here, too, Jesus is the one who perfectly embodies the beatitudes.

Jesus clearly teaches that if we are to be his disciples we have to take on the risk of persecution. In John's Gospel, for example, he says, "If the world hates you, know that it has hated me before you. If you were of the world, the world would love its own; but because you are not of the world, but I chose you out of the world, therefore the world hates you" (15:18–19). We read a similar passage in the Gospel of Luke, where we learn that acknowledging the name of Jesus will provoke the wrath of the enemies of Jesus and the enemies of his righteousness. Jesus tells his disciples that they must be prepared for this: "When they bring you before the synagogues and the rulers and the authorities, do not be anxious how or what you are to answer or what you are to say; for the Holy Spirit will teach you in that very hour what you ought to say" (12:11–12).

The opposition between Christ and the world (namely all that opposes his kingdom) has been a constant theme throughout history. If we stand up for the values of Christ, we will inevitably meet opposition—and this is as true today as it has ever been. Those who stand up for social justice, for the rights of the poor, for the defense of life, often encounter scorn from the powerful of the earth. Christ's values are those of poverty, service, and humility, yet the world is governed by the forces of wealth, ambition, image, and pride. It's interesting to note that those from whom we encounter the greatest opposition often do not reject Christ directly, but they reject his values—the values of his kingdom. If we are to follow Christ seriously, we must be prepared to meet opposition. Living the values of Christ in modern Western culture will inevitably provoke a struggle.

In spite of growing secular ideas about tolerance and freedom, however, countless men and women are still being put to death for what they believe. We think of people like Maximilian Kolbe (1894–1941), a Franciscan priest who gave his life for a fellow prisoner condemned at Auschwitz, and Edith Stein (1891–1942), a Jewish convert, philosopher, and Carmelite nun who died in the Nazi death camps. These people were put to death because the principles of Nazism directly contradicted the values of Christ. Stein was killed for no reason other than the fact that she was Jewish, like her Master. We think, too, of the Jesuit martyrs of El Salvador (six Jesuits and two lay women who were murdered in 1989 for their defense of human rights and their concern for social justice) and Oscar Romero. They lost their lives not because they were Christians but because they defended Christ's poor. One of the great ironies is that it was probably baptized Christians who put them to death. And we think of Martin Luther King (1929–1968), leader of the American Civil Rights movement, who was slain in 1968 because he stood up for racial equality. His life and ministry were a struggle to give flesh to Paul's words, "There is neither Jew nor Greek, there is neither slave nor free, there is neither male nor female; for you are all one in Christ Jesus" (Galatians 3:28).

The twentieth century reminds us that an authentic church will always be purified by the blood of martyrs. The Second Vatican Council's *Dogmatic Constitution on the Church* speaks movingly of the call to martyrdom: "By martyrdom a disciple is transformed into an image of his Master, who freely accepted death on behalf of the world's salvation; he perfects that image even to the shedding of blood. Though few are presented with such an opportunity, nevertheless all must be prepared to confess Christ before men, and to follow Him along the way of the cross through the persecutions which the Church will never fail to suffer" (#42).

In our modern world, where there is much unbelief and, perhaps even more significantly, much indifference, the blood of the martyrs is a powerful witness to faith. Those who have suffered persecution and even died for their faith raise the question of faith before an unbelieving world. Their testimonies often bring others to faith in Christ and in his Father.

Jesus' sober words—"Blessed are those who are persecuted"—prod us to reflect on our own lives. What are the values by which we are living? If our lives are too comfortable, is that a sign that we are not taking Christ's gospel seriously enough? As someone once asked, "If I were brought to trial for being a believing Christian, would there be enough evidence to convict me?"

Questions for Reflection: *How are the beatitudes "attitudes" for Christian living? Do you find the beatitudes realistic for Christians at the beginning of the third millennium? How might the beatitudes bring you comfort when you suffer? How might you use the beatitudes as prayer?*

Chapter 6

The Corporal Works of Mercy

Feed the hungry.
Give drink to the thirsty.
Clothe the Naked.
Welcome the stranger.
Visit those in prison.
Visit the sick.
Bury the dead.

The corporal works of mercy spell out ways in which Christians are called to serve others. As "corporal" works, of course, the focus is on physical and material needs. The scriptural foundation for the works of mercy is the parable of the last judgment in Matthew 25:31–46, which teaches us that the criterion for our love of Christ is love of neighbor.

The corporal works of mercy are a strong reminder that Christian faith is not just about doctrines or beliefs. Rather, faith has a practical component. We are fully Christian only if we put into practice what we believe. This is what Paul means when he speaks of "doing the truth in love" (Ephesians 4:15).

Feed the hungry
Give drink to the thirsty

Those of us in Western societies live in cultures where diet is an important concern. Many adults, for example, seek to lose weight by carefully monitoring what they eat, as in avoiding fatty foods. Our supermarkets sell every variety of milk, such as half-and-half, whole milk, skim milk, two-percent milk, one-percent milk, and fat-free milk, and clinics such as Weight Watchers and Jenny Craig flourish as people seek to shed extra pounds.

At the same time, however, literally thousands are starving to death—in First World counties as well as in developing nations. In American cities, for example, one daily encounters men and women holding signs that read "Hungry" or "Will work for food," and long lines form outside the doors of soup kitchens and food pantries on a daily basis.

In some Third World countries entire populations are dying of hunger. I recently came across publicity from the Catholic organization called Cafod, which raises money to feed the starving. That material told of the Sudan, for example, a country torn apart by civil war. In the last few years Sudan has been ruled by right-wing extreme Islamists, and Christians in the south of the country have been undergoing systematic persecution. The Cafod literature explains, "In the horror of civil war thousands of children are suffering and dying through lack of food and medical aid. Many of them have already had to watch their parents die. In South Sudan, where the fighting is worst, missionary sisters and priests are coping with huge numbers of refugees. More children arrive daily. Some haven't eaten for a month. A recent eyewitness describes bodies thin as rakes, with heads too large for their emaciated bodies." It is estimated that in Khartoum alone there are more than ten thousand refugee children.

In another piece of literature, Cafod explains about the civil war in Mozambique, where thousands of refugees are starving because civil war makes it impossible to grow crops.

At the same time, the government exports crops because of its international debt. The Mozambique government spends ten times more on interest payments than on health care. As part of the millennium celebrations, Cafod is calling upon governments worldwide to cancel the backlog of debts owed by the Third World's poorest nations by the year 2000.

Lack of adequate water is also a death-producing phenomenon in many parts of the world, especially in Africa— in the Meguet region of Burkina Faso, West Africa, for example. This region has been so affected by drought that the wells of the region have run dry, leaving the population without water for drinking, cooking, basic hygiene, and agricultural needs. Thus they are without food. In this area it falls to women and children to walk many miles to haul water to their villages. Although the people try to dig their own wells, they lack modern means of technology. As a result, the wells often collapse because they are not fortified with cement. Fortunately, a large benefaction from a Catholic donor is now making possible the implantation of cement wells in the region.

These facts remind us that famine is due not only to natural causes but to human sinfulness as well, such as war and the exploitation of poor populations. The fact that people are dying of starvation is largely the result of social injustice. As we saw when we studied the seventh commandment, however, we have an obligation in justice to share the world's resources. When we give money to provide food for the hungry and drink for the thirsty, we are helping to rectify injustice throughout the world. We are helping to redistribute, in an equitable way, the resources of our planet.

The church has always encouraged the practice of fasting, especially during the penitential seasons of Advent and Lent. Fasting has many levels of meaning. On one level, for example, fasting is self-denial. When we fast, our stomachs are empty, and this bodily emptiness reminds us of our spiritual hunger and our dependence upon God. But especially in the modern world, where we live in a global village, it is important to link the small hunger of fasting with the greater hunger of the world—a hunger that is not self-imposed but is inflicted from without, often by unjust structures. Many Catholic churches distribute small rice bowls during Lent, suggesting that the money saved by fasting be collected and given to international agencies for the relief of the starving of the earth.

Some years ago, during the great drought in Ethiopia, George Basil Hume (1923–1999), Benedictine monk and Cardinal Archbishop of Westminster, went to visit the suffering of that country. He related how moved he was by seeing the children with swollen bellies. When one young girl pointed to her stomach and then to her heart, the cardinal was struck by how her gesture pointed to the truth of the matter: The only way to overcome the hunger of the stomach is through conversion of the heart.

The world has enough resources to feed all its people. Only when rich nations open their hearts to the suffering of the poor developing countries, however, will hunger be eradicated. Our alms for the starving can be a small part of the conversion process needed to create a more just world.

Clothe the naked

Nakedness is a physical fact that often has symbolic significance; the person who is naked is literally defenseless. A doctor friend of mine speaks of how patients in the hospital, in their nakedness, reveal their great vulnerability before their nurses and physicians. Those who are naked for lack of resources to buy or obtain clothing are very much among those whom Jesus calls the poor.

One of the most moving examples of riches and poverty is found in Luke's Gospel in the parable of Lazarus and the rich man (see 16:19–31). It is not surprising that we find this story only in Luke, for Luke has a special love of the poor. In describing the rich man, Luke notes that he is clothed in purple and fine linen. Lazarus, on the other hand, is covered with sores. Although nothing is mentioned of his clothing, we can imagine that Lazarus wears nothing more than rags. While the poor man sits daily at the gate of the rich man's house, the rich man does not have eyes to see and the poor man goes unnoticed. For failing to clothe or feed the poor man, the rich man finds himself in the fires of hell following his death. The poor man, we are told, is transferred to the bosom of Abraham.

The corporal work of mercy "clothe the naked" finds many echoes in the Christian tradition. For example, Francis of Assisi (1181–1226), son of a wealthy cloth merchant and founder of the Franciscans, was known for his love of creation and a mystical attachment to Lady Poverty. We can imagine the finery his father would have clothed him in. Francis, however, encountered the poor Christ in a vision and was moved to embrace poverty for Christ's sake. His father, of course, was furious at Francis's change of heart and lack of interest in carrying on the family business. When Francis appeared before the bishop and stripped off his finery until he was totally naked, the bishop proceeded to clothe him with the tunic of a beggar. This scene is movingly depicted by the thirteenth-century painter Giotto (1266–1377), one of the greatest painters of the Middle Ages, in his famous fresco on the walls of the upper basilica in Assisi. Francis divested himself of his clothes as a sign of his detachment from worldly goods and his desire to stand in solidarity with the poor.

Another famous saint in the Christian tradition is Martin of Tours (316–397), a convert to Christianity, bishop, and founder of Western monasticism. While still a soldier of the Roman Empire of the fourth century, Martin encountered a naked beggar along the roadside. Feeling compassion for the man, Martin divided his cloak and gave half to the beggar. Christ later appeared to Martin in the form of the beggar, which inspired Martin to become a Christian. As bishop of Tours, Martin was noted for his acts of charity and dedication to the poor, and his gesture of dividing his cloak became symbolic of his sanctity. We may recall the depiction of this scene beautifully executed in the painting by El Greco (1548–1614), artist born in Crete who created his masterpieces in Toledo, Spain.

In the modern world, the fashion industry remains a symbol of the wealthy of the earth. Only those who are economically well off, however, can afford the clothing of Versace, Ferragamo, Gucci, Calvin Klein, and other cult designers. Royalty and celebrities from all walks of life are pursued by the paparazzi who want to capture photos of these people's latest glittering fashions. The whole world of the modeling industry exploits the bodies of young women and men who are able to exhibit designer clothes. Yet, many of these people, caught up in this world of high fashion, are broken by sexual promiscuity and drug addiction. When the beauty of youth fades, these young women and men frequently experience abandonment and unemployment. They are often forgotten and end their lives in destitution.

Although today we do not often meet men and women who are literally naked, the homeless who sleep on our streets are poorly clothed. They lack warm coats in winter and, being homeless, are unable to wash the clothes they do have. It is not uncommon for parish priests to receive the homeless who are looking for a change of clothing and the opportunity to wash. Mothers living in economically deprived situations or subsisting on welfare often have great difficulty in finding sufficient clothing for themselves and their children. Without a doubt, finding adequate clothing remains part of the plight of the poor.

The Lord Jesus summons us to a two-fold attitude if we wish to be his disciples. First, we are called to simplicity of life. Like Francis of Assisi, we are to reject the "purple" of the rich. We do not want to be measured by the glittering images of high fashion. At the same time, we want to avoid the blindness of the rich man in the parable. We want to see the poor and naked person at our door, because that person's nakedness is a sign of poverty that calls us to manifest the compassion of Christ. The rich man of Luke's Gospel did nothing and so was condemned; the believer who clothes the naked, however, will enter into Christ's everlasting kingdom. As we read so beautifully in the book of Tobit, "Almsgiving delivers from death and it will purge away every sin" (12:9).

A famous image of Mary in the Christian tradition is the one in which she extends her mantle as protection for all her children. In the deepest sense, all of us are naked, defenseless, and in need of the mantle of divine protection. It is fitting that we pray for Mary's intercession for all the vulnerable of the earth. May her mantle cover all those in need and most especially the naked of the earth for whom God has a preferential love.

Welcome the stranger

Part of the Jesuit community's ministry in the city of Rome is the offering of an evening meal and shelter for refugees. During a recent stay there, I was struck by a long line of African men waiting by the side door of the residence for the evening meal. Most of those men were Ethiopians who had fled their own country for fear of physical violence. One Ethiopian said that he had been in Rome for seven years. Continually hoping to seek asylum in Canada, he had yet to receive a visa because he is married and has a daughter—and refugees with families find it particularly difficult to be welcomed by a country in the First World.

The United Nations defines a *refugee* as a person who flees the country where he or she has citizenship because of fear of persecution and physical violence for motives of race, religion, or nationality, or because of belonging to a particular social group or holding determined political beliefs. After the Second World War, world leaders feared a global conflict involving nuclear weapons that would destroy the face of the earth. Fortunately, this danger has diminished, but even with the end of the cold war, the world continues to be threatened with violence. The UN reports at least thirty-nine civilian wars since 1990. As a result of these local conflicts, many people have been forced to flee their homes. One thinks particularly of the Balkans and the situation in Africa, with conflicts in Rwanda, Liberia, and Mozambique. In 1997, the UN reported that there were twenty-two million refugees throughout the world, many of whom have been placed in refugee camps marked by inhuman conditions. Some of the camps themselves have become centers of violence, where one party in a civil war brutalizes members of the other faction. Beyond refugees in the strict sense, there are millions of other human beings who, for fear of being murdered, are forced to leave their homes and villages and flee to other parts of their own country. Although not refugees in the strict sense, these people remain among the homeless. (Statistics are taken from an article by Gianpaolo Salvini published in *Civita Cattolica*, 3555/3556, August 1–15, 1998; pp. 303–314.)

The plight of refugees has been a concern for believers as far back as the Old Testament. "Foreigners" were an ambiguous reality for Jews because they were worshipers of foreign gods; Jews naturally felt hostile to them. At the same time, however, the Jews had bitter memories of their own experience of slavery in Egypt and, later on, of captivity in Babylon. Thus the Old Testament contains references to the care that the Jewish people give to foreigners. In Exodus we read, "You will not wrong a stranger or oppress him, for you were strangers in the land of Egypt" (22:21). Deuteronomy speaks in the same vein: "He executes justice for the fatherless and the widow, and loves the sojourner, giving him food and clothing. Love the sojourner, therefore; for you were sojourners in the land of Egypt" (10:18–19).

American cities are not exempt from the presence of refugees: our own homeless. Who can be unaware of the thousands of people who wonder our city streets begging for alms? There is the all too frequent image of the "bag lady," for example, who carries all her earthly possessions in a few sacks and has no fixed abode. These people sleep in our streets, take shelter in the warmth of the subway, and are often afflicted by psychological disturbances and drug or alcohol abuse.

Given this local and global situation, the corporal work of mercy of welcoming the stranger takes on a new urgency. Our contributions to agencies dedicated to giving relief to refugees and those who are homeless are more necessary than ever.

There is, however, another point of concern for Christians, namely our attitude: Is it one of welcome or hostility? In many Western countries, for example, the fear of the stranger results in the closing of our hearts to these people because we project onto them many of the woes of our modern cities. In many cities of Western Europe there are notable acts of violence committed against immigrants, for no other motive than racism. Those fleeing from their home countries are often given menial tasks for employment—tasks that citizens of the host country are no longer willing to perform. Grosser forms of exploitation, such as the practical conscription of women into prostitution, are not rare. The misery of immigrants and refugees is due not only to lack of charity but also to lack of justice.

It is interesting to note how the Bible links together the widow, the orphan, and the stranger—all representing classes of people who are homeless, who are refugees. Hence, these people are particularly precious in the eyes of God, who loves all without distinction but who has a preferential love for the poor because they have special need of divine protection. The psalmist calls God "Father of the fatherless, protector of widows," and goes on to say, "God gives the desolate a home to dwell in, he leads out the prisoners to prosperity" (Psalm 68:5–6). Commentators note that in speaking of the lonely, the psalmist is thinking of Israel during her time of slavery in Egypt. As God shows mercy to his people in a foreign land, so should the people of God show concern for foreigners in their midst. Such is the background for the long Christian tradition of opening our hearts to strangers. In the light of Matthew 25:31–46 (the parable of the last judgment), Christians see an image of Christ in the stranger, in the refugee, and in the person who is homeless.

The gospel of Jesus calls us to conversion of heart. Jesus finds himself a stranger because he dares to eat with tax collectors and sinners. His practice of siding with the excluded leads him to an ignominious death outside the gates of Jerusalem (see Hebrews 13:12). Following Christ, who becomes a stranger to his own people because of his care for those who are excluded, should lead us to open our hearts to the strangers of our own time. The gospel challenges us to see the face of Christ in the homeless on our streets, in the native Indians whose lands are taken from them, in the immigrants and refugees who knock at our door seeking work and shelter. Jesus, hidden in the foreigner, wants to say to each of us, "I was a stranger and you welcomed me" (Matthew 25:35).

Visit those in prison

Brother George, a member of my community, is engaged in full-time prison ministry. He recently experienced great grief over a young man named Michael who, shortly after being released from prison, died from an overdose of drugs. Although Michael was a good man, a man of faith—indeed, he had just been confirmed—he was an addict and needed rehabilitation. He never joined a program, however, and drugs eventually killed him. Before he died, Michael wrote a letter to Brother George:

> Dear Brother George,
>
> I can't thank you enough. I want to let you know you really helped me through some bad times. Brother George, you brought God back in my life and my family too. I really thank God for you. And you're always in my prayers. I thank you for believing in me. Not many have. Today my little girls call me Dad and it feels great. Thank you!

Your friend,
Mike

Brother George believed in Michael, saw Christ in Michael, and wanted to identify with this man who lived on the margins of society.

In the United States the majority of those in prison (some 1,700,000) are minorities: fifty percent are African-Americans; thirty percent are Hispanic. Almost all have some type of addiction and most come from deprived backgrounds: violent neighborhoods and/or abusive families. It is not just an accident or a free choice that lands them in prison.

Those who do prison ministry bear witness to the fact that the worst thing about being in prison is not just the deprivation of freedom. Rather, life in prison deprives men and women of their rightful human dignity. The system hardly seeks to rehabilitate these persons. Rather, they are treated as non-persons, and shame is a pervasive aspect of their daily lives. In an article titled "The Task of Prison Chaplaincy: An Inmate's View" (*Journal of Pastoral Care*, Summer 1992), David Duncombe writes, "The major spiritual illness of most inmates, especially repeaters, is shame and not guilt. At the deepest level they believe that they are 'no good' . . . this radical sense of being worthless, bad, a 'nothing,' which lies at the root of most antisocial behavior, is the spirit of evil which broods over the place of imprisonment."

When men and women arrive in prison, they are stripped naked and their bodily cavities are searched in a humiliating way. They lose their personal name, are given a number, and are then moved into vastly overcrowded quarters—cells that were originally designed for one person that now house four. The toilet in the middle of the cell stands as a monument to how prisoners are stripped even of their right to basic privacy.

The prison ministry of Christians is an attempt to recognize the dignity of these human beings. In spite of their crimes, which can be quite heinous, they are still God's creatures and the object of God's love. As Brother George says, "I am not there to judge them but to listen to them." Christians are called to minister to those in prison to testify to their worth. If the prison system exists for the purpose of punishing criminals, prison ministry exists to remind criminals that the God of Jesus does not want the sinner to die but to turn to the Lord and live.

In spite of the great grief that Brother George felt at the death of Michael, he is hopeful. He writes, "I have felt the power of Christ's love and compassion in Michael's story, and I am deeply consoled that I was able to offer him the chance to express that love for God in his life." This is the corporal work of mercy: to let those in prison know that God does not abandon them and that Christ is with them, even in this most degrading of human situations.

Visit the sick

One of the obvious dimensions of the ministry of Jesus is healing the sick. Early in the Gospel of Mark, for example, we are presented with the story of the paralytic who so desires to see Jesus that he is lowered through the roof of the house to get close to him (see 2:1–12). Jesus displays the divine power he possesses by curing the man and telling him to take up his mat and walk. At the same time, Jesus makes it clear that this physical healing is only a sign of something greater. Before offering to cure the man's physical infirmity, Jesus says, "Your sins are forgiven." The connection between the two is important, because in the Bible physical sickness is always associated with death and sin.

In the beautiful poem of Zachary, later to be known as the Benedictus, Luke portrays humankind as walking in the shadow of death (see 1:68–79), and there is no clearer evidence of this shadow than physical infirmity. Human sickness points to the fact that we are mortal and will, in fact, die. As

Paul teaches in the letter to the Romans, death came into the world through Adam (see Romans 5:12); sickness points to death and death is the ultimate manifestation of sin. When Jesus cures our infirmities in the body, he is symbolically pointing to our greater need of redemption from sin.

Although the Gospels portray Jesus as a healer, they are aware of a great danger in this understanding. For example, people could conceive of Jesus' mission in a magical way, looking to Jesus as a wonder worker. Rather than seeing him as the Lord who calls us to conversion, humans could seek for relief from suffering without any willingness to change their lives. The Gospel of Mark, therefore, tellingly plays down the cures that Jesus performs. Those who are cured, in fact, are admonished to silence. Mark continually points to the mystery of the death and resurrection of Jesus as the miracle *par excellence*. The ultimate way to overcome sickness, death, and sin is to participate in Jesus' death and resurrection. Christians are summoned to die with Jesus so that they can rise with him. The way to eternal life passes through death not around it.

Being sick is a manifestation of our living in the shadow of death. Weak and vulnerable, those who are sick need to be cared for, often in their most primitive needs such as being washed and fed. Being sick can be humiliating, for when we are sick, we are not in control of our lives. There are many stories of those dying from AIDS, for example, whose emaciated bodies—covered with sores and continually subject to diarrhea—have been cared for by friends. The demanding process of cleaning the body is a sign of great fidelity on the part of loving relatives and friends. Those who suffer with AIDS live Paul's theology of the cross: "My power is made perfect in weakness. . . . When I am weak, then I am strong" (2 Corinthians 12:9–12).

In 1999 John Bayley, a professor of English literature at Oxford University, published *Eulogy for Iris*, a moving memoir about his life with his wife, Iris Murdoch, who had a brilliant career as a philosopher and novelist and who had been suffering from Alzheimer's disease since the mid 1990s. In the last months of her life, Iris was completely incapacitated and looked out at reality with a blank stare that every now and then was illuminated by the flash of a smile. She no longer recognized others and did not always recognize her husband. She appeared to be like a child of three. Yet, John ministered to her, gave her constant attention, and offered her his protecting presence. One can hardly imagine a greater sign of love.

In an earlier section of this book, we reflected on the church's sacrament of the anointing of the sick, which offers a share in the healing presence of Christ, both physically and spiritually. Visiting the sick is a ministry of presence. As we attend to the sick, we care for their bodily needs. But recognizing how sickness reduces a person to vulnerability, and recognizing how illness can often isolate a person, we offer first and foremost the great gift of our presence.

When I was a young priest and graduate student in Germany, I had the privilege of bringing communion to the sick. At that time, I had only a limited ability to speak German and so my ministry was curtailed. As I made my communion calls in the small village in which I lived, I would often see groups of young people motorcycling about or congregating in the village square or sports field. These people exhibited a great joy in being together. Then I would enter into the homes of the sick, where the elderly were often totally isolated from the life of the village just outside their doors. Although an elderly spouse or adult child may have been caring for them, I was overwhelmed by their isolation. I felt so privileged to be there with them and to bring them the presence of Christ. Even without the gift of words due to the language barrier, I was able to mediate for them the presence of Christ. It was truly a humbling ministry.

Anyone who has ministered to the sick, especially those who are gravely ill or dying, knows that words often fail. What can we say to those who are suffering so acutely in the shadow of death? What do we say to the relatives? What words are adequate to comfort family members whose husband and father and brother and son and friend is being preserved in life only by machines that must eventually be turned off?

Not long ago there was the terrible massacre that occurred in Northern Ireland when the IRA set off a bomb in the center of the village of Omagh. Because the bomb went off at the height of the shopping day, many were killed, including women and children. What do we say to the survivors in the moment of burying their dead? As one reflective journalist observed, surely the answer is "Nothing." No words can suffice. But then again, no words are necessary. It is sufficient to be there with the survivors—silently. And perhaps our very silence names the Unnameable: the Mystery of God.

Jesus promises ultimate victory over sickness, suffering, and death. In the meantime, our presence with the ill and the dying points to the presence of Christ and to the hope that his dying and rising instills in our hearts.

Bury the dead

I am reminded of a quiet summer day when I received a phone call from a local funeral home looking for a priest to lead a service for a man who had died of AIDS. The man wasn't a Catholic but had intended to become one. His friends told me that he loved God, had a special devotion to Mary, and wanted to be buried with a rosary in his hands. Although there was only a handful of people at the service, I have rarely felt more a Christian or a priest than when I carried out the Lord's injunction to bury the dead in that experience.

One of the most beautiful scenes in the Gospels is the one in which Jesus meets the widow of Nain. She has recently lost her only son and has no husband or other children. She is a portrait of one of the poor of the earth—alone, indefensible, defeated.

This scene, recorded only by Luke (see 7:11–17), so typically reveals the compassion of Jesus. It is curious that in introducing the scene, the Evangelist immediately calls Jesus "Lord," the title indicating his divinity and hence his sovereign power over death and the forces of chaos. Luke tells us, "When the Lord saw her, he had compassion on her and said to her, 'Do not weep'" (7:13). Then he raises the young man from the dead and returns him to his mother.

This gospel passage reveals the compassion of our God who takes pity on a humanity that "sits in darkness and in the shadow of death" (Luke 1:79). It also gives a word of consolation and hope to all of us who are destined to die. Every one of us, at some point, is like the widow who loses a loved one. Every one of us, at some moment, is like the young boy who lies upon the bier.

When we practice the corporal work of mercy of burying the dead, we do what Jesus did: We take compassion on the suffering of those around us—of the family and friends of the loved one who has died. We stand in solidarity with them in their grief. There is very little we can do; we cannot change the situation or bring the dead to life. But we can be with those who have been left behind. We can console them with our presence.

Burying the dead with faith is a "remembering" before God—and there is no more characteristic act of the Bible than remembering. The Jews "remember" their deliverance from Egypt, and the first Christian communities gathered to "remember" the Last Supper of Jesus. In the Christian rite of burial we remember the life of our dead brother or sister. It is God who has given life and it is God who now takes the person to himself. We acknowledge this fact and give thanks for that life. We remember all that the dead person has been and done—who he or she has been for family, friends, and the Christian community. In remembering all of this, we also give thanks to God.

Because the corpse has a special relation to the person, the burial is also an act of reverence for the body. The person has expressed his or her personal reality through that body, thus the corpse is not just a decaying composition of chemicals. Rather, it is the earthly remains of the person and, as such, is entrusted to the earth as its place of rest. In this act, we express our hope; from the earth the dead will one day arise, when Christ returns in glory. Burying the body of a beloved brother or sister is truly an act of piety and reverence toward that person.

In burying the dead we also pray for the deceased. From earliest times the Christian community has believed that death does not finally separate us from the one who has died. Rather, we are still bound together in the body of Christ. Our prayers for the deceased help that person on the journey into God's kingdom and aid the purification necessary so that the dead can finally see God face to face. In hope and trust we commend our dead brothers and sisters to God's mercy. We pray that God will forgive their sins and bring them into the everlasting life of his kingdom.

We also console ourselves, not only with the consolation of our presence to others in the time of grief, but more radically with our faith in the resurrection. In celebrating a Christian burial we remember Paul's words in his first letter to the Thessalonians: "We would not have you ignorant, brethren, concerning those who are asleep, that you may not grieve as others do who have no hope. For since we believe that Jesus died and rose again, even so, through Jesus, God will bring with him those who have fallen asleep" (4:13–14).

Burying the dead without hope of victory over death is, indeed, a daunting task. I have personally presided at funerals where the relatives and friends lacked faith and, truly, they were inconsolable. But Christians bury the dead with the sure hope of the resurrection. We carry in our hearts the comforting words of the Preface for the Dead: "For your faithful people, Lord, life is not taken away but changed." This hope gives us strength not merely to survive the death of a loved one but to keep living in the fullest sense of the word. In the context of faith, this corporal work of mercy is, therefore, closely linked to Christ's words in the beatitudes: "Blessed are you that weep now, for you shall laugh" (Luke 6:21).

Questions for Reflection: *What parallels do you see between the Ten Commandments and the corporal works of mercy? Do you see opportunities to practice the corporal works of mercy in your life? In what areas are national policies severely lacking respect for the corporal works of mercy? How might you influence your national leaders to incorporate the corporal works of mercy into their policy making?*

Epilogue

The criteria for Christian living can hardly be summed up in a simple formula, but I do offer three words that can serve as keys for understanding our faith: *love, surrender,* and *communion.*

All of Christian faith is about *love*: God's love for us in Christ. The author of the first letter of John says, "God is love" (4:16). He also underlines the important truth that the great miracle of God's revelation is that we have not taken the initiative toward God but rather, it is God who has loved us first (see 4:10).

In the early centuries of the church, the community's struggle to grasp this truth led to the understanding of God as Trinity; God and Trinity are the same. God is not merely a first principle or cause; rather, God is the love of the Father and the Son and the Holy Spirit, a love that has been open to us from all eternity.

God's love for us is expressed simply but beautifully in a few words from the late medieval mystic Julian of Norwich (1342–1420), author of the *Book of Showings*: "Our soul is so preciously loved of him that is highest, that it passeth the knowledge of all creatures, for there is no creature that is made that may fully know how much, how sweetly and how tenderly that our Maker loveth us."

Once we know that love, what can we do but *surrender* to it? And this is the mystery of faith—not so much a "believing that," but a loving surrender to the God who is love. Faith is surrendering to God each day of our earthly pilgrimage.

Finally, God is the eternal *community,* and God wishes nothing less than to unite us with him in communion. Here on earth, we Christians are in communion with him, for we have his Holy Spirit dwelling within us. Each day the Lord Jesus offers us this communion again when he comes to us in the flesh in the holy Eucharist. Ultimately, we hope that we will be united with the Trinity in an everlasting communion of love when we come to our Father's home in the kingdom.

As Paul says: "So faith, hope, love abide, these three; but the greatest of these is love" (1 Corinthians 13:13).

For Further Study

Balthasar, Hans Urs von. *Credo: Meditations on the Apostles' Creed*. New York: Crossroad, 1990.

____. *A Short Primer for Unsettled Laymen*. San Francisco: Ignatius Press, 1985.

Bonhoeffer, Dietrich. *The Cost of Discipleship*. New York: Macmillan, 1959.

Catechism of the Catholic Church. London: Geoffrey Chapman, 1994.

Duffy, Eamon. *The Creed in the Catechism: The Life of God for Us*. London: Geoffrey Chapman, 1996.

Hellwig, Monika. *The Meaning of the Sacraments*. Dayton, Ohio: Pflaum/Standard, 1972.

____. *Understanding Catholicism*. New York: Paulist Press, 1981.

Kasper, Walter. *The Church's Confession of Faith: A Catholic Catechism for Adults*. San Francisco: Ignatius Press, 1987.

Keenan, James F. *Commandments of Compassion*. Franklin, Wisconsin: Sheed & Ward, 1999.

Kelly, Liam. *Sacraments Revisited*. New York: Paulist Press, 1998.

McBrien, Richard. *Catholicism*. San Francisco: Harper and Row Publishers, 1994.

Macquarrie, John. *Principles of Christian Theology*. London: SCM, 1977.

O'Donnell, John. *The Mystery of the Triune God*. London: Sheed & Ward, 1988.

_____. *Prayer in the Catechism*. London: Geoffrey Chapman, 1995.

Osbourne, Kenan. *Sacramental Theology: A General Introduction*. New York: Paulist Press, 1998.

Ratzinger, Joseph. *Introduction to Christianity*. San Francisco: Ignatius Press, 1990.

Speyr, Adrienne von. *The Countenance of the Father*. San Francisco: Ignatius Press, 1997.

Index

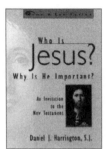

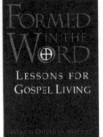